CATALINA

JIM WATSON

A Channel Catalina Publication

To my Mom and Dad, nephew Johnny and…

To the wanderers and adventurers: all times, all places.

CONTENTS

PREFACE

In January of 2011, I started a column in the weekly *Catalina Islander* newspaper called "Mysterious Island" named for one of my favorite Jules Verne classics, *L'île Mysterieuse*, or "The Mysterious Island." The film *Mysterious Island*, released in 1961 (the year I was born), has long been one of my favorite Saturday afternoon matinees-type films. Never did I dream in those days that one day I would live on just such an island.

The column began as a journal of sorts to chronicle one of most overlooked yet most fascinating aspects of life on Catalina Island, namely the Island's historical oddities, legends and myths, or—as I like to say—Catalina's "facts, folklore and fibs."

This book represents a sizeable portion of my ongoing research into the Island's history and culture that I have pursued over the 15-plus years I have lived here, jotting down notes, making trips into the hills and interviewing locals and visitors alike. These accounts—real, imagined or just plain made up—are stories that are unique to an Island that has variously gone under the names Limu, Pimu, San Salvador, Isla de Juan Rodriguez, Isla Capitana and Santa Catalina over the centuries.

There is the story of a UFO filmed by a U.S. Navy photographer over Blackjack Peak on a clear spring day in 1966. There are accounts spanning more than 20 years of what law enforcement officials and eyewitness wildlife experts—including a Woods Hole biologist—have described as a genuine black panther prowling the hills.

There are wild tales of inexplicable phenomena occurring in the scrub oak canyons of Toyon Bay and tales of restless spirits wandering the hills of the interior and the halls of your friendly neighborhood bed & breakfast.

There are not-quite-fully-explained historical oddities of a more earthly nature as well, such as the elusive answer as to just exactly why the bison were brought to Catalina. There are tales of the Silent Film era when Catalina was Babylon-on-the-Pacific, including the mysterious death in 1924 of director Thomas Harper Ince, whose untimely demise occurred on a yacht whose passengers (some would say suspects) included none other than Charlie Chaplin and William Randolph Hearst.

Sharing the pages of this book with tales of the supernatural are stories of Spanish shipwrecks, English pirates, Nazi war criminals and Indian antelope, all taking up memory on the Hard Drive of Catalina history.

The purpose of this book is not to convince anyone of the existence (or non-existence) of ghosts, UFOs or multi-dimensional portals, but rather to simply highlight the unique folklore—real or imagined—that has evolved here.

Among those I wish to acknowledge in helping me compile this book include my mother and father, who breathlessly awaited my next writing or drawing project as a child, including my early "works" on dinosaurs, snakes and sailing ships; Chuck Liddell, native-born Islander and tireless "bearer of the torch" of Catalina's history and folklore; my brother Fritz, with whom I made my first trip to Catalina in 1987; Dan Teckenoff, former publisher of the *Catalina Islander* who helped me get this whole idea off the ground; Dr. Bill Bushing for his level-headed scientific approach; and Ron Pyke for his sage input during our frequent conversations on Front Street.

Others who deserve special mention, including those who tipped me off to many of the mysteries in this book include Lolo Saldana, Joe Katin, Jennifer Leonhardi at the *Catalina Islander*, Vince Bodiford and Dennis Kaiser, also at the *Islander*, Paxson Offield, Sean Brannock, Doug Bombard, Don Salvo, Hannah Hoffman, John and Kathleen Cummings, Kathleen Bergen for her artistic assistance, Kristy Throndson, Mark Tasca for assorted "insider" information, Greg Wenger, Dick and Nancy Kellogg, Jim Parrish, Jim Gilligan and Colleen Hernandez.

J.W.
July 4, 2012
Avalon, California

INTRODUCTION

A mere seven leagues south by southwest of the Palos Verdes Peninsula lies a world that is stranger than fiction; a storied land where the lines between fact and folklore, logic and legend are blurred beyond all recognition. Like *The Lost World* of Sir Arthur Conan Doyle, it is a land out of time and out of place.

It is a land where the realm of the natural blends seamlessly with that of the supernatural; a place where the real and the surreal cheerfully share the same niche in time and space against all the rules.

Twenty-one miles from Los Angeles across the impetuous, often malicious San Pedro Channel looms a wayward land of legend and spectacular beauty; a land unimpressed with the march of the centuries; a mysterious island that the world has come to know as Santa Catalina.

"People sometimes ask me if the hotel I manage on Catalina is haunted. I tell them I never cared much for the word 'haunted' and instead prefer the old-fashioned term, 'enchanted'.

"This hotel is 'enchanted'," I tell them.

"This whole island is 'enchanted'."

—Hotel Manager in Avalon, 2006

The Ghosts

OF AVALON

Many of Catalina's ghost stories have been around for decades and are well known to locals. Footsteps, slamming doors and wispy apparitions pervade the homes in Avalon and more than one hotel guest has spent an uneasy night in the safety of the lobby, daring not go back into their room after an encounter there.

The Ghosts of Avalon linger. They watch us. And they wait for the day, when we will join them.

THE GHOST IN THE GRUMMAN GOOSE

To paraphrase the Bard, there are more mysteries on Catalina Island, Horatio, than are dreamt of in your philosophy and it is well known to anyone who has spent any length of time here that ghost stories abound on the Island.

But an incident that occurred in the late 1940s instructs us that they can sometimes be found in the skies as well.

Robert Hanley made a local name for himself during the post-war years as a pilot for Amphibian Air Transport and Avalon Air Transport. In the late 1950s, he was the owner and operator of Catalina Channel Airline, an enterprise that lasted nearly a decade.

In a book titled *Ghosts of the Air: True Stories of Aerial Hauntings* written by Martin Caidin, Hanley writes a guest piece about a nerve-wracking, and ultimately mysterious, event that took place in the late 1940s when Hanley was flying for the old Amphibian Air Transport.

It was on a cool autumn day when Hanley and ten passengers slowly climbed into a Grumman Goose G-21 from the airport in Burbank bound for Catalina through the low cloud cover surrounding the nearby Hollywood Hills.

It was the last flight of the day, but trouble started early when Hanley emerged from the clouds only to notice cars on the highway ABOVE his plane along a nearby ridge. "Just climb higher REAL soon," he told himself. And so he did.

But the new altitude brought its own problems in the form of ice, which rapidly began coating the plane's radio antenna. The ice didn't stop there, however, and soon his entire windshield was covered with it, making it impossible to see anything ahead of the plane.

The tension was eased considerably after Hanley finally got the Goose above the cloud cover. But although he now had good visibility out the side windows, he realized that the cloud cover now obscured all of the ground below. "That cloud cover, now below us," he wrote, "was absolutely flat as far as the eye could see. Not a lump anywhere."

Then, things got a whole lot worse when the ice building up on the antenna suddenly broke away, taking the whole antenna with it. Hanley and his passengers were now several thousand feet in the air with cloud cover between them and the world below and no way of communicating with those on the other side of those clouds.

No problem, thought Hanley to himself. "Fly your airplane, dude," he told himself.

Using an old pre-radar pilot trick, he counted the minutes, knowing that it was 20 minutes from Burbank to Long Beach and another 17 minutes from there to Catalina.

After 30 minutes, he began easing the plane lower, bit by bit, calculating that by now he was over the open channel, approaching the Island's leeward side. They descended lower and lower until they were swallowed up by the clouds. Would the Goose and its occupants find open sea below them? Or would they plow directly into East Peak or Mt. Orizaba?

He was now well on his descent on a heading of 180 degrees when a "voice" clearly spoke to him, he writes. "Turn to nine zero degrees," said the voice. *"Turn now!"*

It took Hanley a moment to realize that he still had his headphones on; headphones that blocked out the voices of anyone in the plane; headphones that—because of the missing radio antenna—were completely and utterly useless. And yet he had heard the voice.

Hanley obeyed the mysterious command and rolled his Goose 90 degrees. Immediately, the plane broke through the clouds at 900 feet right into the middle of mountainous terrain. "Hills and mountains loomed all about," he wrote, "under and to the right of my wingtip."

Within minutes, as Hanley tried to figure out just exactly where he was (had he circled around somehow and was back over the mainland?) he looked directly below the nose of the airplane and saw Avalon. After a nail-biting half hour, Hanley safely landed his plane and its passengers.

Hanley would later discover that the "absolutely flat" cloud cover was flat only because of a 70-mile-an-hour wind, which had pushed his plane much further along than he had reckoned. These winds, he calculated, would have almost guaranteed that—without making the 90-degree turn—he would have plowed his plane and all of its occupants straight into Mt. Orizaba, the highest peak on Catalina Island.

"I didn't hit the mountain because a voice in dead earphones, when I was flying absolutely blind, told me to 'turn to nine zero degrees. *Turn now!*'

"Where did that voice come from?," he asked himself. "That's where I run out of answers. The whole thing seemed impossible, but I'd heard the voice, and I obeyed it."

Robert Hanley has long since passed from this earthly plane and his earthly planes. But without the "Ghost in the Grumman Goose" that passing could have occurred much earlier.

THE GHOST OF CRICKET ALLEY

While many of Avalon's ghost stories are rooted in age-old traditions handed down through the decades, not all of them are confined to the past.

Such is the case with that little nook of a cranny we call Cricket Alley at 125 Metropole Street that houses a number of small establishments, including our Radio Shack/Catalina Discount & Variety store.

According to two of the former employees at that location, there was a period of about a year or two when they regularly saw the apparition of a "young man" passing not only through the corridor that links all of the little shops in Cricket Alley, but on at least one occasion within the store itself.

On a number of occasions, Maria Mulgado and a fellow employee watched as this vision walked by the front windows of the store only to disappear behind the separation in the store's front windows or behind advertising posters. The employees—clearly aware that what they were seeing was not a normal, living soul—immediately ran to the front door into the corridor only to find nothing—and no one—there.

On one frightening occasion about two years ago, Maria and another employee were preparing to open the store in the morning when they noticed a young man inside near the back of the store between some merchandise displays. Disturbed by the thought of someone in the store before operating hours, they both walked over to the area.

The man was nowhere to be found until Maria looked back at the cash register area only to see the "man" crouching behind the counter. When they ran over to the counter and looked down, the man was gone. Those who know the layout of the store know that even David Copperfield couldn't have pulled off an escape without being seen.

A few months later there was another sighting in the outside corridor, but since then the employees have told me they have had no other experiences.

Who could this intruder from "beyond" be? The employees claim that nothing was unusual about the man's attire or hair styles. In other words, he didn't appear to be from any particular era.

Unfortunately for the ghost hunting crowd, the history of the property doesn't shed much light on our mystery.

The building surrounding Cricket Alley dates back to the late 1800s—not unusual for Avalon—and having been primarily a hotel over that past century was certain to have seen a great deal of human drama.

Roger Upton, who owned the property for the better part of 15 years, is probably the number one authority on its history, yet he doesn't recall any unusual events or any sordid histories that might account for our ethereal visitor.

Upton actually bought the building from the original owner, Harold Stamford, "years and years ago" and oversaw not only the Hotel Stamford which occupied the building's upper floors, but the ground floor-based Catalina Hardware Store, a Catalina fixture (pun intended) for many decades.

One of the more interesting historical tidbits of the building concerns the bullet it dodged in 1915. "It's one of the few buildings that lived through the fire of 1915," said Upton. "Harold (Stamford) was up on the roof all day keeping it from burning down."

But Upton doesn't recall any accounts of paranormal activity and eventually sold the building for more earthly reasons. "The reason I sold it is because I got tired of listening to all the noise and the operation of the hotel," he said. "That business was an old, old hotel without any bathrooms in the rooms."

It's been over a year now since any reported sightings of the Ghost of Cricket Alley. It remains a mystery who our visitor was and just exactly what he was up to—or when he might return.

GHOSTS OF THE CASINO

No other building on Catalina Island stands out more than the fabulous Avalon Casino, so it's no surprise that innumerable tales of ghostly encounters surround the structure.

Built in 1929, the Casino consists of a movie theater (best described as a movie *palace*) on the ground floor and what's billed as the world's largest circular dance floor at the balcony level. In between and all around these magnificent chambers is a labyrinth of side rooms, storage rooms, hidden crawl spaces and lengthy, confusing corridors.

Many of the stories of sightings revolve around the Mezzanine level between the downstairs theater and the upstairs ballroom, specifically the area around the women's restroom on the building's west side.

Long-time tour guide Chuck Liddell recalled an episode that occurred several years ago when his 16-year-old nephew Arthur, also a tour guide at the time, was playing "tail end Charley" on one of the day-time tours. It was Arthur's job to follow behind the tour group to make sure no one lagged too far behind or tried to hide someplace.

As Arthur's tour was finishing with the group heading back down the ramps to exit the building, Arthur noticed a "middle-aged man" with an old-fashioned camera hanging around his neck. The man was dressed in the typical tourist garb of the 1950s, with Bermuda shorts, sandals with socks, and a bright Aloha-style shirt.

Arthur informed the man that the tour was ending and that he needed to exit the building. The man didn't seem to acknowledge Arthur's presence and said nothing to him in response. In fact, the strange tourist seemed to be looking "right through" Arthur, he said.

The man then turned and walked into the women's restroom with Arthur in pursuit.

Well, maybe he just needs to use the restroom, thought Arthur to himself, even if it was for the wrong gender.

Arthur decided to stand guard at the entrance to the restroom—the only entrance *or* exit—and wait.

After about 20 minutes, Arthur grew impatient and went into the restroom to look for the man, who was nowhere to be found. This sent the young Arthur into a near-panic and he ran home where, according to Chuck, he was hysterical.

After much consolation, "Uncle Chuck" was finally able to convince Arthur to finish up the season and continue working in the building.

On another occasion, a friend of mine named Brian was walking past the same women's restroom with another employee of the building when they distinctly heard the disembodied voice of a woman yelling "get out!" They did.

Brian told me this story one day while we were both walking by the restroom. Just the retelling of this story was enough to make Brian *run* for the exit, even though it was several years after the incident.

While most of the building's well-known ghost stories revolve around the Mezzanine level, the theater area on the building's ground floor nevertheless has its own tales to tell.

Chuck Liddell, mentioned earlier, has one of the most profound—and confounding—experiences of all the Casino's employees.

It all started one day as he awaited the start of another tour he was to lead. He was standing at the snack bar in the lobby when he first noticed a man walking in his direction out of the corner of his eye. Since there weren't any other tour guides around and the tour group had not yet been allowed into the building, Chuck turned around to face the man.

Before he could utter anything to the stranger, the man literally *walked right through the wall* separating the lobby from the inside of the theater. This was something he saw straight on, not out of the corner of his eye.

Even stranger, or perhaps appropriate, Chuck noticed the man's attire was decidedly old-fashioned—*very* old-fashioned—dating back to about the World War I era or perhaps the early 1920s.

What's interesting about the period of the clothing is that the modern-day Casino was not even built until 1929. Its precursor was known as the "Sugarloaf Casino" and had a much more open interior than today's Casino. Therefore, it's highly likely that there was no wall in that particular location back then.

A couple of friends of mine had another unnerving experience in the theater's lobby. Dave and Linda had just entered the lobby from the theater after watching a movie when Linda went into to the sitting area of the women's restroom to freshen up in the mirror.

Dave contented himself with sitting and waiting on one of the vintage couches lining the lobby's black walnut-paneled walls.

When Linda emerged from the restroom she was as white as a sheet.

"Did you just see a ghost or something?," joked Dave. It turned out his "joke" was no joke at all.

Linda then related to him how she had been brushing her hair in the mirror when, only two feet from her, the "translucent" figure of an elderly woman in a long white robe *floated* by her and out into the lobby.

Evidently, no one else saw the apparition enter the lobby, so perhaps the spirit only allowed Linda to see her.

The experience was somewhat traumatic for Linda, who—like many non-believers who have a paranormal experience—instantly became a believer.

Who was this ghostly woman? Theater employees and Island residents have long told stories of an elderly woman haunting the women's bathroom area. Normally, there is no exchange of information or even acknowledgement of the presence of the living on the part of the spirit.

Some, however, have reported the woman sometimes asks "Where is my husband?"

A young girl of about five or six, the daughter of an island resident, once said this ghostly woman appeared to her and bent over to whisper in her ear "Where is he?"

Is this the spirit of the same woman who haunts the women's restroom on the Mezzanine level? To date, no one knows who she is, or for that matter, who her "lost" husband is.

"SANDRA'S" TALE

Another Avalon ghost story involves a friend of mine we'll call "Sandra."

Years ago, she told me one of the most harrowing ghost stories I've ever heard; a terrifying tale that, nonetheless, has a fascinating and "happy" ending.

It was about six years ago that she moved in with her then-boyfriend into one of Avalon's old, old homes—the ranger's house at the Hermit Gulch Campground.

As the newcomer to the house, she was paid a rather disturbing visit in the middle of the night by what was evidently a very long-time resident: "I woke up in the middle of the night," said Sandra, "and there was a woman staring me in the face telling me to get out!"

The woman kept yelling at Sandra, telling her she was "not welcome" in the house. Just like in the movies, efforts to awaken her snoring boyfriend lying next to her were, of course, in vain.

Sandra said that the woman was clearly ghost-like in her appearance, without color and a more or less translucent body. She had no accent and appeared to be a white woman in her thirties or forties.Needless to say, our local gal was unnerved by the event and, of course, couldn't get to sleep again all night.

Sandra told me over the course of the next few weeks she would catch glimpses of the apparition drifting through the halls of the old place until finally one night she was paid another visit.

This time, however, the "ghost woman" awakened her from a more civilized distance a few feet away and announced to her that she had "been wrong" about her and that Sandra was, in fact, welcome to stay.

I'm sure she felt much better after that.

RISTORANTE DEI FANTASME

In case your high school Italian isn't so good, or if your high school didn't even offer Italian, the title of this segment roughly translates to "The Haunted Restaurant."

As you may have surmised, this particular restaurant—the Ristorante Villa Portofino on Crescent Avenue—is one of our several Italian restaurants in Avalon and one of my favorites on the Island.

But aside from the delicious *Scampi al Vino Bianco* and the incredible *Luna Piena di Pollo*, the restaurant holds another fascination for me: it just happens to have some of Avalon's most astounding ghost stories.

Teresa Brizuela has worked at the Portofino for more than a decade. She most often works alone during the morning hours, cleaning the restaurant and the kitchen area.

Her first, but certainly not the last, experience occurred shortly after she began working in the place. At about 5 a.m. one early morning, she was fetching a mop in a cleaning storage area near the kitchen area. Suddenly, only five feet away from her, she saw a man walking down the stairs into the basement. Teresa was naturally startled by the man's presence since the restaurant was closed and all the entrance doors locked.

She walked towards the man and watched as he literally disappeared before her eyes.

"You mean he went around the corner and disappeared?," I asked.

"No," she said. "He disappeared, *desaparecio*, before my eyes."

Nearly hysterical, she screamed at the man in both English and Spanish. "Who is it?! *¿Quien es?,*" she demanded.

She grabbed a heavy steel wrench from some nearby CO_2 bottles and boldly descended the stairs down into the basement through the only entrance or exit. There, she looked in each of the tiny storage rooms and around the ice machine, but there was no one to be found.

She described the man as being a shorter, balding middle-aged man. He appeared to be wearing a baseball-style cap along with a sports team-style jacket.

Some time later, Teresa was cleaning the floor tiles at the entrance to the kitchen area. Her back was turned to the front windows of the restaurant through which early morning light was illuminating the interior. As usual, she was alone.

Suddenly, she noticed a large shadow cast itself over the floor and the wall in front of her. Remembering her earlier experience, she first counted to "three" and then turned around to see *un hombre como una sombra* ("a man like a shadow") moving through the restaurant and disappearing into the nearby busboy's station.

Other employees, too, have seen this same figure descending into the basement, a place that many of the kitchen workers refuse to enter when they are alone.

One former employee remembers sitting in the office in the kitchen late one night and seeing someone walk right by the office door. Since no one was supposed to be in the building at this hour, the employee immediately rose and looked out the office door to see who the trespasser was, only to find no one there.

So who is our spectral friend? Given that the building has been there for many decades, it could be just about anyone who was ever associated with it: former owners, managers, employees, devout patrons who just couldn't leave this earthly plane without knowing whether or not *torta di granchio* was offered on the "other side."

Such spiritual "hangers-on," I am told, are often those dear departed individuals who had the most emotional attachment to the particular locale they are haunting, and one of our prime candidates may be Vincent Scarimucci, who owned and operated a restaurant there for many years named, appropriately, "Scari's Restaurant."

I spoke with several locals who used to know Vincent and although the clothing description of a baseball-style cap and jacket didn't sound familiar to them they said the general description of a shorter, balding middle-aged man is an exact match.

Teresa has had no cessation of encounters with this spirit since her original one several years ago. In fact, glimpses of the "shadow man," as well as plates scooting off tables by themselves and even physical brushes against someone "who is not there" have become so common she now laughs them off.

"I think it's funny, now," she said. "Whoever he is, he is here and I don't care anymore."

TALES FROM THE TOYON

Toyon Bay, located a couple of miles or so north of Avalon, has long been the focal point of peculiar, mysterious tales going back nearly a century. Among them is an old ghost story that used to circulate around the crackling campfires beneath the diamond stars at the old boys' school there.

Back in the 1920s when the school operated, the headmaster and his wife lived in a modest cabin at the top of the ridge overlooking the canyon. The story goes that the wife had always wanted a daughter (in part to balance out her life among boys) and in these pre-ultrasound days was disappointed, to say the least, when she gave birth to a baby boy.

One day the young boy was playing around a nearby cliff when he slipped and fell. Grabbing on to a nearby tree branch, he called for his mother, who came racing to the scene. Rather than help the poor boy, and keeping in mind her self-promise of having a daughter, the mother backed away and watched as the toddler fell to his death.

In time, the wife became "with child" again and, hiding her terrible secret from her husband, hoped for a baby girl. Her dream was fulfilled when she gave birth to just such a bundle of joy.

The wife's happiness, however, was short-lived, for in a few years the young daughter found herself slipping from the same cliff and dangling from the same tree branch.

Responding to her daughter's cries for help, the mother once again raced to the scene. As the mother stood poised to help, the daughter yelled out "Are you going to save me *this time*, mommy?"

With that, the young girl plunged to her death.

Insane with grief and guilt, the mother locked herself in the little cabin and burned the building to the ground—with her in it.

The ghost component of this story should be obvious, of course, with tales of the spirit of "mommy dearest" haunting the area that, curiously, became known over the years as "the Shrine"—a name it still has to this day. All that remains of the structure is the stone fireplace and chimney.

As quaint as this story is, it was but the precursor to other, more compelling—dare I say more terrifying—stories that emerged over the years.

Dr. Bill Bushing has been a well-known fixture around Avalon for more than 30 years. The "doctor" part of his moniker is the result of a Ph.D. in biology from Harvard. He has been a part-time professor at UC Santa Barbara and is well-respected in his field.

When Bill first moved to California he landed himself a dream job as a senior faculty member at Toyon Bay, which had since become home to the Catalina Island Marine Institute.

Bill told me one of his experiences at the camp from the autumn of 1969:

"I am a scientist. I don't know if these were ghosts or not, but I can't explain what happened," he said.

It seems that Bill and a friend of his, John, were sitting around their little bungalow one evening. John had returned earlier from a camping trip up on the ridge near the Shrine.

Suddenly, Bill noticed that the room "got really cold." It was then that Bill noticed that John had flopped on his back and "went into a trance." He began mumbling in what sounded to Bill like a foreign language. While the words were unintelligible to Bill, it was clear that John was "talking to someone else."

After a few minutes, John snapped out of it. He then sat up and asked Bill, "Did you hear that?"

"John, I heard *you*," replied Bill. "You were mumbling or talking or something."

"It was the spirit," said John. "It was the spirit I met when I was camping up at the Shrine. It was telling us that something is going to happen in this room, but that we shouldn't be afraid."

Confused and a little amused, Bill got up to make a trip to the fridge. He had barely gained his footing when suddenly "the whole house started shaking," he said.

"I fell to the floor," he said. "I couldn't stand up. All the windows had come undone and were flapping open and closed. I had no idea what was going on."

As it turned out, the shaking was nothing more than an earthquake—something with which Bill as a new arrival to the West Coast was unfamiliar. But the mystery of the story, of course, is not in the quake itself, but rather in the warning that preceded it.

Was this a warning from the old school master's wife perhaps fulfilling some karmic obligation to atone for her horrible sin?

But this experience was only the beginning for Bill. On another occasion, shortly after the quake warning, Bill had returned from the Safeway store in Avalon with a load of canned and dry goods. He set the box of groceries on the kitchen floor in his cottage and did what I would have done under the circumstances: lay down to take a nap.

Shortly thereafter, he was awakened quite suddenly by his own pet cat clawing at his chest. "And there was this box of groceries," he said, "moving across the kitchen floor.

"I continued to watch and it continued to move until it was across the room," he said. "I thought this was really weird."

It got even weirder when Bill watched as the box slid back across the floor nearly to the place it had started. "No one was there to touch it," he said.

But the weirdness was just beginning. As a senior faculty member, one of Bill's jobs at the camp was to patrol the grounds at night, making sure trash was picked up, the right doors were locked, and so on. It was during some of these security patrols that he reported seeing "blue and white humanoid shapes" drifting around in the distance, floating "a few feet above the ground." He described the beings as having leg-like and arm-like appendages.

These unnerving and unexplainable events may have something to do with one of the time-honored legends of Toyon Bay: the Green Door, which is discussed later in the book under the chapter "Quantum Catalina: UFOs and Strange Portals."

THE TRUE STORY OF THE TOYON BAY SÉANCE

I purposely saved the best ghost story for last, here in our chapter of Catalina ghost stories; a story that, in my opinion, tops the list of the most terrifying paranormal tales in Island lore.

I had long heard stories of the infamous séance at Toyon Bay a mile north of Avalon that occurred in the winter of 1969 and was always curious about following up on it. I had also noted that the story has a vast amount of credibility to it, to wit, one of the participants and witnesses present was Mr. Paxson Offield.

For Islanders, "Packy" (as he is affectionately called) is a man who needs no introduction. But for the benefit of the visitor who may read this column, Packy is descended from the Wrigley Family and ably headed the Santa Catalina Island Company for many years.

He has been a spearhead of environmental and philanthropic causes over the years, including the Offield Center for Billfish Studies and the International Game Fishing Association, as well as the local drug intervention program, CHOICES.

He is as sensible as any a gentleman who has led commerce and industry, and as honest as any a fellow who has sailed salt water.

"I was not expecting what happened," he told me one day from his home in northern Michigan regarding the séance. "It happened and it really shook me, to say the least. It shook me up pretty good."

In that rainy winter of 1969, some friends of Packy's—fellow students at the Catalina Island Marine Institute at Toyon Bay—happened upon a human skull that had evidently been washed out of its not-so-final resting place into a ravine. Their first mistake was bringing it back to camp.

Their second mistake was trying to contact its owner.

It was decided by the group of four friends, including Packy, that a séance would be held and preparations began for the event. The first thing they needed to find out was just exactly how one holds a séance.

"There was some information that we were able to garner from the library in Toyon at the time," he said. "Most of the time we had to go overtown (to the mainland) for the information."

A number of months went by while they prepared for the event, but finally the fateful day—or more correctly—night arrived. It was decided that the séance would be held at midnight in the old boathouse on the beach, complete with black candles and, of course, the guest of honor—a human skull that they took to be Native American.

The first run-through of the séance produced no results. Disappointed, the group began the process again. This time, the results were almost immediate.

First, the temperature in the room dropped sharply and the black candles suddenly went out. Within minutes, a glowing blue-white sphere of light entered the room through a closed window and passed out through a closed door.

Suddenly, the young man who was leading the séance sucked in a massive breath and began speaking "in a foreign language." Although he could not identify the language, Packy said it was not simple gibberish. "It was a structured language," he said.

The other boys watched in amazement as the "channeler" continued rambling in this foreign tongue, puffing great clouds of steam into the suddenly-frigid air as he did so. Incredibly, the boy then began to levitate with his legs still crossed from sitting on the floor.

Once in the air, the young man was then hurled across the table, over the skull, and right on top of a startled Packy.

They all bolted from the building and reconnoitered out on the beach to try to make sense of what had just happened. It was then that they noticed that the boy who had been possessed, as it were, was having trouble breathing.

Despite his breathing problems, the séance leader bravely returned to the boathouse to collect the skull. He then placed it in the closet of his cabin. They then all went back to their cabins for the night to try to get some sleep.

The night passed uneventfully, however, in the morning the boy's breathing had become so labored and serious they decided that they had to get him to the hospital. There, despite the doctor being unable to find anything medically wrong with the boy, the situation worsened. "He had a really tough go of it that night," said Packy.

The young man literally was clinging to life throughout that first night in the hospital and it was then, during that long night, that a fire spontaneously and mysteriously ignited in the boy's closet back at Toyon right next to the skull itself.

In the words of Thomas Magnum, I know what you're thinking. The next order of business would be to get the skull out of the camp and back to the place where it was found—which is exactly what they did. It seemed to work, for there were never any disturbances from that point on.

Taking into account that Packy had "a healthy amount of skepticism" before the séance, what were his subsequent thoughts and beliefs regarding the paranormal?

"I think the world is becoming much more open to thinking that way," he said. "We're not just looking at it one way anymore. It's through a different prism that we're looking at the world these days."

While cautioning against anyone trying this experiment at home ("I don't recommend anybody doing a séance") he summed up his Toyon Bay experience thusly: "If you're agnostic and you need an experience to indicate that there is life after death, you need to have an experience like that."

Criptids

AND OTHER MYSTERIOUS ANIMALS

Like most regions of the United States, Catalina Island has its share of criptids, or mysterious animals. Seemingly out of time and out of place, these critters range from our iconic buffalo to inexplicable sightings of panthers, sea monsters and, yes, even Bigfoot.

THE CATALINA "BLACK PANTHER"

Catalina Island is home to a wide variety of animal life ranging from our iconic buffalo (okay, bison) and white-tailed deer, to our darling little foxes and untamed shrews.

As we all know, many of these animals are not native to the Island and found themselves here only by means of introduction via the Island's only bipedal mammal, *homo sapiens*.

There are many mysteries surrounding these introduced animals (particularly humans), but for now I will deal with an exotic beast that many claim to have witnessed wandering the hills of the Interior over the years: a genuine "black panther."

To begin with, let's get one thing straight: there is no such thing as a "black panther" per se. "Black panthers" are really nothing more than otherwise normal members of the large cat family that have a case of what's known as melanism, or a genetic darkening of the fur and skin.

Even the term "panther" is something of a misnomer, since it is derived from the Latin classification *panthera* and applies equally to lions, tigers, leopards and jaguars (but not bears).

While black South American jaguars get the lion's share of publicity in the "black panther" department, African leopards and North American cougars (a.k.a. mountain lions) have also been known to exhibit this anomaly. Though rare, sightings of "black cougars" in Southern California are not unheard of.

But Catalina Island has never been known to harbor any members of the large cat family, much less melanistic ones. And yet...

Dr. Bill Bushing recalls an incident from the 1970s when he lived and worked at Toyon Bay northwest of Avalon. A visiting biologist from Massachusetts' prestigious Woods Hole Oceanographic Institution came running up to his unit one day and asked if there were any "large black cats" on the Island.

Bushing, who himself holds a Ph.D. in biology from Harvard, said the man had been walking by the old tennis courts at Toyon when he saw such a cat standing up at a nearby drinking fountain lapping up water from the fountain's basin.

"I told him what I knew about the black panther," said Bushing, adding that he personally had never sighted such a beast on the Island.

The biologist then led Bushing to the drinking fountain. "There in the mud," said Bushing, "were two large, fresh paw prints." The "cougar-sized" prints," he said, "were much bigger than a feral cat."

Over the years, Bushing said numerous others had claimed similar observations, including a group of biologists from USC and even an L.A. County Sheriff's Deputy.

But sightings are not confined to long-passed decades, and sightings have been reported in recent years and even months. Something to think about the next time you're sleeping under the stars at Ben Weston...

Local musician Butch Azevedo recalls a memorable day only a few years ago when he was out in the Interior doing some oak sapling monitoring near the Laura Stein Volunteer Camp. While taking a lunch break, he said he and the other members of his group spotted a large black cat pacing around at a distance of about 200 yards.

"It was not a deer, it was not a buffalo, it was not a regular cat. This thing was huge, probably 200-plus pounds," he said, swaying his shoulders back and forth in panther-like fashion.

In the summer of 2008, J. Gilligan was at Little Harbor Campground searching the beach area for the wayward children of some fellow campers when he came face to face with a large black cat in the dark of night.

While walking along the Whale's Tale, the rocky prominence that juts out into the middle of the harbor, he pointed his flashlight to his left and spotted the critter only a few feet away from him. "The light was on the cat and the cat was looking at me," he said.

While he has ruled out that the cat was a mountain lion, it was nevertheless one special cat indeed, he said. "It was not a panther," he said. "I'd call it a genetic freak of nature," saying it was probably in the 20-pound range and came up about knee high.

During that same summer, he encountered several hunters from Arkansas staying at the same campground who reported a similar experience and asked Gilligan if there were any "black panthers" on the Island. Gilligan told them his tale.

Just last summer, Colleen Hernandez was working at the front desk of the Glenmore Plaza Hotel when she was approached by two couples who were staying at the hotel with a tail tale of their own.

"When they came back from their stroll," said Hernandez, "one of the gentlemen asked if we had panthers or mountain lions on the Island."

Growing up on Catalina, Hernandez had heard occasional rumors of sightings of black panthers on the Island, but never with any specifics. She related this to the guests.

The four then told her they had seen what they believed to be a "black mountain lion" pacing along the hill near the Casino, no less.

When it was pointed out to the guests that the area is a gathering place for feral cats and that what they saw may have been a rather large specimen of same, one of the men responded with a decisive "no," adding that they all lived in mountain lion country and knew the difference well.

"He was positive it was not a regular cat," said Hernandez. "He said the way it moved and the size of it, that's how they were convinced."

In the words of Thomas Magnum, I know what you're thinking. How could such a critter possibly exist on Catalina? In the 30 million years or so since Catalina first hung out its shingle, the Island has never been connected to the mainland, not even for a few minutes. Furthermore, the span of the San Pedro Channel has always been considered an impassable barrier to the dispersion of large land mammals.

For the record, Carlos de la Rosa, former Chief of Conservation & Education for the Catalina Island Conservancy, said his organization has no record of any reports, much less evidence, of large members of the cat family on the Island, a scenario he says is "very unlikely."

"Any of the biologists who have been here for a long time don't put much credibility in this story," he said, adding that people who have reported sightings were probably seeing something much tamer, such as a large feral cat or perhaps a pet dog.

"There are a number of black feral cats up to 15 to 20 pounds in the Interior," he said. "Possibly they saw one from a distance."

Our porcine friends may be another explanation, according to de la Rosa: "Five or six years ago they might have seen pigs," he said, "because some of the pigs were actually black," he said.

If, however, for the sake of argument, we say that at least some of the sightings of a black mountain lion are indeed accurate, the most plausible explanation would be that, somewhere along the line, an exotic pet owner on the mainland grew tired of having his slippers, newspapers and Plymouths chewed up and decided to rid himself of "Whiskers" or "Eldridge" or whatever he called his pet black panther.

A person owning such an animal would presumably be of some financial means and might have access to a vessel large enough to transport the animal to Catalina; a thoughtless act that would obviously put many people in danger.

Such insensitivity gives one paws.

Problem is, given that the average life expectancy of a cougar in the wild is only about 8 to 12 years, this wouldn't explain the span of decades of reports, unless of course (Heaven forbid) there's a whole pride of them out there breeding...

CATALINA'S "NESSIE"

"Mystery of waters, never slumbering Sea!"
— James Montgomery

Ask the average person on the street to name a few of the most legendary, elusive and mythical(?) beasts in the history of humanity and far and away the survey would say "Bigfoot" and "the Loch Ness Monster."

No other criptids have captured the world's imagination, at least in Western cultures, to a greater extent than these two big lugs.

In the next segment, I cover Catalina's only reported Bigfoot sighting, but the waters around Catalina at one time were the location of a number of sightings of perhaps our very own "Nessie."

The sightings occurred many years ago and all of the principals involved have long since passed from this early plane. But the number of sightings and the distinction and prestige of those involved make for a fascinating bit of local lore.

Named not for the town of San Clemente, but for the Island of the same name, the Clemente Monster was first reported in the early 20th century.

"It had a great columnar neck or body," claimed author and attorney Ralph Bandini on a fateful fishing trip off Catalina in 1916. "Surmount this neck or body with a flat-topped, blunt reptilian head."

Bandini went on to describe the eyes as "two huge, round, bulging" ones—features that would be common to subsequent sightings.

"Two things stood out above all others," continued Bandini. "Those enormous eyes and its unbelievably huge bulk. I never want to look at such eyes again."

In the June 1991 issue of *National Fisherman* magazine, Bandini elaborated on his sighting. "It was as big as a submarine, like something out of prehistoric times." In this 1991 version, he also claims to have fired a number of shots at the beast with his 30-30 rifle; an act which had the desired effect of sending the critter scurrying into the depths.

Most of the sightings of the Clemente Monster occurred during the 1920s, including a close encounter in 1920 or 1921 by none other than George Farnsworth, after whom Farnsworth Bank off Catalina's windward side is named.

"Whatever it was," said Farnsworth, "(it) stood 15 to 20 feet out of the water...I seized the glasses and had a perfect view because we were running towards it."

"Its eyes were 12 inches in diameter, not set on the side like an ordinary fish, but more central. It had a big mange of hair, about two feet long," he said. "I saw it afterwards several times," he continued. "Lots of people said it was a sea elephant. Well, I know a sea elephant...This was no sea elephant."

Was this Mr. Farnsworth's sneaky way of keeping others out of his fishing grounds? If so, he apparently enlisted the help of several others over the years.

One of the Tuna Club's most famous early members, George C. Thomas III, described as "not given to tall tales or exaggeration" reported a sighting in the mid-1920s; an encounter that appears in the book "History of the Tuna Club."

"What the hell was that?," asked Thomas of his fishing partner upon seeing "a big black form, like the sail of a Japanese albacore boat." As they approached the creature, it submerged out of sight.

The last recorded sighting of the Clemente Monster (that I could find anyway) took place in 1927 off the Orange County shore. Howard Wilson, the Orange County editor of the *Los Angeles Times* in those days, claimed to have seen our seafaring friend about 400 yards off Laguna Beach.

He claimed the "brownish" monster had a camel-like head and neck, along with "eyes like dinner plates and a neck that extended some ten feet above the surface of the sea."

Now, in the 21st Century—whether from our waters or from our minds—the Clemente Monster has apparently moved on.

BIGFOOT!

They've gone by various names over the ages depending on what region of the world they are reportedly seen: Sasquatch, Yeti, Ts'emekwes, Yawee, etc. But the most common moniker that rings a bell in the mind of the average American is the name "Bigfoot."

We've all heard of Bigfoot. Not all of us have had the pleasure of meeting him, or her, or them, but we certainly are familiar with tales of their legendary-ness.

Although accounts of the baldness-challenged, eponymous creatures can be found dating back to ancient times from cultures spanning the globe, reported sightings really began in earnest as early as the 1920s and were given a big leg up with the release of the famous Patterson-Gimlin film footage purportedly of a Sasquatch taken in Bluff Creek, California, in 1967. (Many years later, one of Patterson's buddies 'fessed up, claiming that the footage was actually of himself parading around in an ape suit).

As far-fetched as the idea of Bigfoot sounds, I was surprised to learn that the most famous primate researcher of them all, Jane Goodall, recently expressed her belief on National Public Radio in at least the possibility of their existence, a phenomenon she said she found "fascinating."

But what does this have to do with Catalina Island? I'm glad you asked, because as it turns out, Catalina has not missed out on the fun, because it seems that in the Fall of 1987, a gentleman by the name of Peter Hameline claims he had an encounter with Bigfoot right here in Avalon Canyon—Hermit Gulch Campground to be exact.

In his official report to the organization known as Bigfoot Encounters, Hameline said his encounter happened while passing the golf course in the dark of night while making a foray into town for a six-pack of beer when he began to hear a "repetitive, almost inaudible moaning/breathing sound."

The sound grew louder and louder, he said, and after a quick prayer or two he continued on his way. "There's not a soul around," he said to himself. "This place really shuts down at night."

All was well until he passed the stables when suddenly the horses "freaked—and I mean freaked!"

The horses bolted in his direction, stopping just at the fence line, where he got a good look at their flaring nostrils, wide eyes and pinned-back ears.

He then looked down the road and saw "a human silhouette roughly 6 ft. tall."

Hameline got a better look as the creature began running parallel to the road through the golf course. "The color of its body was either brown or a reddish brown all over," he said. "Its strides were smooth and efficient."

"As the arms pumped rhythmically with each stride," he continued, "the open hands snapped back and forth in their curled position. The upper body was erect and leaning forward slightly."

According to Hameline, the creature then ran along the golf course parallel to the road at a speed of "20 to 25 miles-per-hour" before disappearing into the darkness.

I would like to have talked with Mr. Hameline about his encounter, but his whereabouts are not known at this time. He appears to have been something of a Bigfoot researcher himself, although whether his encounter on Catalina turned him into one or whether he just happened to already be a Bigfoot researcher ahead of time is unclear.

I did, however, catch up with another Bigfoot aficionado by the name of Bobbie Short who interviewed Mr. Hameline about his Catalina experience.

"I personally interviewed Peter 10 years ago," said Short. "I felt at that time that his description was valid," he said. "I believe Hameline passed away some years back so I don't know exactly what to tell you except you are welcome to paraphrase the story in your own words."

I won't bother to theorize about how Bigfoot could make it out to Catalina Island, let alone how one could survive out here without holding down at least two or three jobs.

It suffices to say it is just another drop in the fascinating bucket of lore we have in this Island Paradise.

THE BUFFALO RIDDLE

If ever there was a mystery on Catalina Island, a mystery that evades solution and yet involves a facet of life here that is ever-present and even iconic to our lifestyle, it is the question of just exactly how the buffalo got here.

For decades, the prevailing wisdom—the folklore, if you will—has been that Catalina's *bison bison* were originally brought to the Island in 1924 for filming the Zane Grey classic *The Vanishing American*, a Famous Players-Lasky Corporation film released in 1925.

The reference nearly always cited for this belief is an article that appeared in the December 24, 1924, *Catalina Islander*. The article does indeed state that a herd of 14 buffalo were brought to the Island "in separate crates" and dropped off at the Isthmus where it was "quite possible" they would be used in an up-coming Lasky film. But there is no mention of the name of the film.

The mystery begins with the fact that the 1925 version of *The Vanishing American* does not contain any buffalo whatsoever and, on top of that, shows no terrain that even remotely resembles Catalina. For the record, the Internet Movie Database does show Catalina Island as being one of the filming locations, and it's certainly possible that the animals were filmed for the movie but ended up on the cutting room floor.

The trail took another twisting turn when I came across a brochure from the mid-1950s at the Los Angeles Public Library that stated that "a stock of 13 (bison) was brought to the Island by John White, foreman of Middle Ranch, after being filmed in the western *The Covered Wagon*.

(*The Covered Wagon* was another Lasky western released in 1923, but was not filmed on Catalina. This reference to the film was bolstered by Bud Upton in a *Los Angeles Times* article on Catalina Island printed in the 1970s).

The key word in the sentence from the brochure is the word "after"—meaning that the movie (buffalo included) was not filmed on the Island, but may have been brought over after the film was in the can.

It just so happens that the Catalina Island Museum has a copy of *The Covered Wagon*, so one fine day Ron Pyke and I pulled up a couple of chairs at the Museum Research Center on Metropole Avenue and watched the whole thing and, yes indeed, there were lots and lots of buffalo in it.

Was Catalina Island the next destination for these mammalian movie stars after the wrap party? And were they brought out with at least the intention of filming them in *The Vanishing American*, even though it appears Catalina was never used as a filming location for that film?

The search for the answer to the origins of Catalina's buffalo has been a long, dusty trail worthy itself of a Zane Grey tale. If the buffalo themselves know the answer as to just exactly why their ancestors were brought to the Island, they aren't talking.

THE ELUSIVE BLACKBUCK

"Criptid. Noun. An animal whose evidence or survival is disputed or unsubstantiated, such as the yeti," according to the Oxford Dictionary of the English Language.

The woods are full of animals that may not exist and in previous stories we've explored two notable criptids reportedly seen on the Island over the years.

But our Island is graced with yet another mysterious, elusive beast known as the Blackbuck antelope or, to Caesar, the *antilope cervicapra.*

Okay, so the Blackbuck of Catalina don't really qualify as criptids, but they're darn close to it. There is no doubt that they exist and they are seen, albeit on rare occasions, from the patio of the DC-3 Gifts & Grill at the Airport-in-the-Sky.

Carlos de la Rosa, former Chief of Conservation & Education for the Catalina Island Conservancy, traces the introduction of the Blackbuck to a fledgling plan to turn Catalina into a big game hunting preserve back in the 1970s.

This plan, according to newspaper accounts at the time, was to involve the construction and operation of a hunting lodge near the airport and was expected to accommodate up to 6,000 hunters annually.

"One male and two female Blackbuck antelope were introduced to Catalina in 1972," said de la Rosa, adding that the population never really grew like that of the mule deer.

"There are very, very few left," he said. "It's an anomaly. They never really became established permanently."

Blackbuck antelope are indigenous to the Indian subcontinent, particularly to the province of Kannada, India, where they are known as Krishna Mriga.

They are among the fastest animals on earth, reaching speeds of up to 50 miles per hour, meaning that—stamina and terrain notwithstanding—one could theoretically race from Two Harbors to Avalon in about 12 minutes.

The evolution of this kind of speed is understandable considering their most common predator was the now-extinct Indian cheetah.

One of the species' more unusual traits, at least for antelope, is that the males and females have distinctly different colors, making the job of biologists much easier to do from afar.

They even play a role in the Hindu religion. Known as Krishna Jinka in some parts of India, the Blackbuck is thought to be the vehicle for the moon goddess Chandrama. According to the *Garuda Purana*, the Blackbuck bestows prosperity wherever it roams.

And what will be the fate of these antelope that roam on Catalina where the deer and the buffalo play (or something like that)?

"They will disappear on their own," said de la Rosa, "in a few decades."

"When you only have a couple females and maybe one male, they become inbred and that weakens the animals and they will not be successful," he said. "That is obviously not a population that can sustain itself."

Because the animal is not native to the Island, there is no intention of introducing additional individuals to supplement the herd.

So for the time being, our little "ghost herd" of a handful of females and one lucky male will be free to live out their days, contentedly grazing in their outdoor retirement home on the California Riviera.

Free from the predators that lurk behind the shrubbery of their ancestral homeland, they will nevertheless fade away one day into becoming yet another Catalina legend.

THE GREAT WHITE TERROR

They are found in all of the oceans of the world, so there is no escaping these fellows, even in the waters around Catalina Island.

Being epipelagic in nature (meaning they prefer the upper, sunlit reaches of the open sea), the Great White shark (*carchorodon carcharias*) is most commonly found in the earth's temperate zones, wherever the water is about 55 to 75 degrees Fahrenheit.

That range of temperature covers a lot of territory, including South Africa (where they are found most abundantly), the Atlantic Seaboard, Australia and, of course, both Northern and Southern California.

The first thing that people need to realize is that, despite what you've seen in the movies, human beings are decidedly not the preferred food of great whites.

They greatly prefer seals and a variety of larger fish. In fact, most of the human deaths attributed to Great White attacks are the result of the beast simply "tasting" the unfortunate victim before spitting him back out. Unfortunately, this taste test often severs vital blood vessels and since the victim, being out in the ocean and all, is often a long ways from help it often ends badly.

While there are numerous examples of fatal Great White attacks in Southern California over the past century, there has never been such an event recorded in the waters around Catalina.

For the most part, these predators prefer either the East End around Seal Rocks or the entire backside of the Island, far from human habitation and the buzz of Evinrudes and Tohatsus.

There have, however, been some mighty terrifying encounters...

Dr. Bill Bushing was kayaking around the Island with a buddy back in the 1970s. They were doing a counter-clockwise circumnavigation and about half way through found themselves off Ben Weston Beach on the Island's windward side.

They were enjoying the fine, sunny summer day when a helicopter appeared out of nowhere and began buzzing them.

At first, Bill and his friend waved at the chopper, which they took to be just paying them a good-natured visit. But the helicopter stayed and got lower and began flying erratically—and uncomfortably close—to them.

"What the heck is this guy doing?," asked Bill.

After a few minutes of this increasingly bizarre activity, the chopper then pulled away and disappeared back over the hills.

It wasn't until Bill's trip was concluded and he was back in Avalon when he bumped into the pilot of the helicopter.

"So what was that all about, when you were buzzing us out at Ben Weston," asked Bill.

The answer chilled Bill to the bones: "You guys were being followed by a 14-foot Great White. I was trying to scare him off."

Only last summer, JoJo Machado was fishing off the East End for white sea bass, as he has done regularly for the past 20 years. It was late afternoon when he saw a fin breaking the sea surface. "I saw the fin and thought it was a seal," he said. "Then I see it make a turn and I said 'that's no seal'."

The mystery creature then hit his 40-lb. test line and took off. "It snapped my hook," he said. "It snapped my rod holder."

After the rod holder broke, the culprit made a turn and came at his boat. It was then that he saw clearly it was a Great White that was nearly as long as his boat. "My boat's 18 feet long," he said.

The shark came alongside and merely nudged his skiff before disappearing into the deep.

His brother Bobby had a similar experience several years ago, except that Bobby was just getting ready to actually jump into the water before seeing a similarly-sized Great White come barreling just underneath the boat.

One of the most terrifying, as well as most recent, encounters (a bloodless one, fortunately) took place only two years ago near Eagle Rock on the windward side of the West End.

On the morning of June 21, 2008, Bettina Pereira was kayaking in that locale while her husband Andrew and their son sat on their nearby 50-foot yacht. About 500 feet from shore, Bettina felt a knock on her kayak. She thought nothing of it at first, until she saw the dorsal fin coming right at her.

The fin ominously slipped into the water just before the shark slammed into her kayak, knocking her and her watercraft into the air.

Bettina then came down—landing FEET FIRST—on top of the shark.

Fortunately, this seemed to be enough to startle the beast: the shark took off one way and Bettina took off the other way, giving her crucial time to distance herself from her attacker.

"Mom fell off the kayak," her son told her husband back on the yacht.

Husband Andrew was just then thinking it strange that the experienced kayaker would have a mishap when their son caught sight of the nearby dorsal fin: "Oh my god! There's a shark after her!," he yelled.

Lucky for Bettina, two other nearby boats raced to the scene in less than a minute. They successfully plucked her from the perilous waters, leaving her with the ability to one day tell this story to her grandchildren.

quantum catalina

UFOs and Strange Portals

Catalina Island has long been considered a hotbed of UFO activity, with some UFO researchers going so far as to say there is a huge undersea UFO base in the channel between Catalina and mainland. Sightings are numerous and some of the most famous UFO film footage ever taken was captured at Blackjack Peak in the Island's interior in April 1966.

THE CATALINA-ROSWELL CONNECTION

On July 8, 1947, a remarkable headline splashed across the front page of a small town newspaper in the dusty, relatively unknown town of Roswell, New Mexico.

It seems that the crew at the public information office of the nearby Roswell Army Air Field reported they had recovered wreckage from a "flying disc" that had crashed near a ranch outside of town. The *Roswell Daily Record* duly reported it, sparking an event that the world would come to know as "The Roswell Incident."

The following day, General Roger M. Ramey of the U.S. Army's Eighth Air Force, stated that—rather than an exotic disc-shaped craft—his men had, in fact, recovered the debris from a wrecked radar-tracking balloon. A press conference was held—complete with a display of the alleged wreckage—and, satisfied with this, the press went on their merry way.

Not as widely reported at the same time, however, were a number of other "disc" sightings both before and after the Roswell incident.

On the evening of June 26, 1947, U.S. Army Major George Wilcox of Warren, Arizona, reported a series of "eight or nine" disc-shaped objects traveling near his home and at an altitude of about 1,000 feet above the nearby mountains.

That same evening, a Captain E.B. Detchmendy reported seeing a "white disc glowing like an electric light bulb" passing over Pope, New Mexico, a sighting echoed by several local townspeople.

Dozens of other sightings—many by military officers—were reported in the region in the coming days and weeks.

But the Southwest wasn't the only venue. Similar sightings were reported throughout much of the western United States as far north as Washington State and as far west as California—including Catalina Island.

On July 8, 1947, the very same day that Roswell's *Daily Record* was reporting the initial "flying saucer" story, a remarkable incident reportedly occurred in the skies above Avalon. An article on the front page of the week's issue of the *Catalina Islander* details an alleged sighting by three visiting Army veterans of six "flying discs" traveling at high speed from the northeast and passing directly over Avalon before disappearing over East Peak.

According to the story, the six discs appeared at about 1 p.m. and flew in a formation of two sets of three and were witnessed not only by the veterans, but by "hundreds" of others as well.

Alvio Russo, one of the reported witnesses and an Army Air Corps veteran who had flown 35 bombing missions over Germany with the Eighth Air Force, estimated the velocity of the discs at "850 miles an hour," according to the story.

Bob Jung, listed as a "former aerial photographer" agreed with this estimate and said they were flying roughly as fast as the U.S.

Navy's "Tiny Tim" rocket, which he had photographed numerous times for the Navy.

In the coming months, the sightings of discs around the nation waned, at least for the time-being, and public interest in them faded as well. Even the Roswell Incident was largely forgotten until 30 years later when famed ufologist Stanton Friedman began fielding what he claimed were eyewitness reports from civilian and military personnel of REAL flying saucer wreckage and alien bodies.

No mention of the Catalina incident was ever made again in the *Catalina Islander* nor, apparently, in the *Los Angeles Examiner*.

As far as the local hub-bub was concerned, the aliens-over-Avalon story seems to have faded as quickly as those inexplicable discs disappeared over the vast Pacific Ocean.

THE BLACKJACK UFO

On a lovely Spring day in April of 1966, a Mr. Leland Hansen was performing some aerial photography work for the U.S. Navy near White's Landing when he spotted what appeared to be a shiny, cylindrical object speeding along the ridge near Blackjack Peak. He quickly turned his camera to the object and filmed it for several minutes.

The film was later released with narration and has since been seen in numerous television programs and UFO documentaries over the years, from the aforementioned "UFO Hunters" episode to Leonard Nimoy's old *In Search Of…* series from the 1970s. (This footage is readily available for viewing on YouTube by simply searching for "Catalina UFO 1966.")

As the film begins, the voice-over claims that "You are seeing an Unidentified Flying Object. It is real. It is not a hoax."

It then goes on to state that the film "has been examined by photographic experts. Photographic analysis reveals this circular UFO was about 30 feet in diameter and was traveling between 130 and 170 miles per hour."

As we see the object drifting by Blackjack, the narration concludes with "Mr. Hansen also observed this object hovering stationery in the air before it began to move."

At least one prominent scientist and author, no less than Arthur C. Clarke of *2001: A Space Odyssey* fame, put the film to his own test and came to the conclusion that the object was nothing more than a single engine Piper Cub airplane. Clarke revealed this in an episode of his own series television series *Mysterious World*.

According to Clarke the wings and tail section of the plane "can plainly be seen" in the blown-up version.

Many, however, disagree with Clarke's findings and the infamous Blackjack UFO film still pops up from time to time. While dozens of other UFO sightings have been reported on the Island over the decades the Blackjack footage lives on in Catalina folklore.

THE CASINO UFOS

The stretch of water between Catalina Island and the mainland, known as the San Pedro Channel (often erroneously referred to as the "Santa Catalina Channel"), has long been a hotbed of UFO activity.

Sightings of triangular-shaped craft, flying discs and strange lights at night are common and seem to come in waves. A year or even several years may pass with no sightings when suddenly there are dozens of reports, sometimes in a single night.

Just as common in the area as UFOs are USOs or "Unidentified Submerged Objects." In fact, USOs around Catalina were the topic of a popular Discovery Channel documentary several years ago.

UFO researchers, quaintly known as "ufologists," theorize there is a vast submarine extraterrestrial base in the waters around Catalina and that the sightings are nothing more than the comings and goings of their craft.

Some of the many UFO sightings in the channel include:

In October of 1968, a man named George Hiner was fishing in his boat off of Catalina's East End when he witnessed a "white dome-shaped object" through his binoculars. The object rose about 10 feet above the surface of the ocean. It descended once again, but then rose for a second time.

Suspended beneath the object was a strange parachute-like apparatus. The object then slowly slipped back into the sea and disappeared.

In 1970, a man was sailing from Catalina to San Pedro when he saw a "metallic saucer" with four "hemispherical pods" beneath it flying only a few hundred feet above his boat.

In 1990, a flying instructor named Toshi Inouye was flying with a student pilot over Santa Monica Bay when they witnessed a glowing cigar-shaped object hovering near their plane.

"It was standing still in the air, glowing red," said Inouye. "We were kind of stunned. We didn't know what to do."

Inouye was about to call a nearby airport control tower when the object suddenly shot out of sight.

But 1992 was a particularly active year for sightings in the channel with reports made by dozens of people including law enforcement officers. Independent witnesses reportedly claim seeing "in excess of hundreds of USOs" all over the San Pedro Channel as far north as Malibu.

The USOs, they said, emerged from the water and hovered in the air for a short time before shooting up into the sky at incredible speeds in complete silence.

It was only a few years later, during the summer of 1998, that a bizarre sighting occurred on Catalina.

Catalina Islander Chuck Liddell was returning to Avalon from nearby Pebbly Beach with a couple of friends one unusually hot summer night when they became witnesses to one of Catalina's most extraordinary UFO sightings.

The trio of tour bus drivers had just parked their rigs at the tour company's facilities south of Avalon and were walking back to town along Pebbly Beach Road.

"We were coming around Abalone Point when we saw this very bright green light above the road to the Zane Grey Hotel," said Chuck. He described the light as being oval in shape.

He then said out loud, "That's strange. There's no tower there or anything." At first he thought it might be a car headlight, but then realized there was no road where this light was located.

The three men stopped in their tracks to gaze at the light when it suddenly started moving. The light drifted from its position on the hillside straight over the top of the Casino where it came to rest "about 30 or 40 feet above the cupola."

Things only got stranger when the single light was suddenly joined by four other similar green lights. The five lights aligned themselves above the Casino—and then it *really* got weird.

All three men watched in fascination as the five lights then began doing a "carousel" type of up-and-down movement. "They were all going up and down," he said, "but the first, third and fifth lights would go up while the second and fourth lights were going down," said Chuck.

This bizarre dance—in seemingly perfectly controlled movements—continued for a while until finally the lights lined up once again and one by one shot straight across the channel towards the mainland and then out of sight.

THE STRANGE "BACKSIDE LIGHTS"

Most regions of the country have, as part of their folklore, tales of "mysterious lights" that appear to lucky observers from time to time.

Known collectively as "ghost lights," these phantasms are assigned paranormal causes by some, but written off by scientists as the spontaneous ignition of swamp gases or the atmospheric refraction of distant campfires, car headlights and even porch lights.

There is the "Paulding Light" of Michigan's Upper Peninsula, said to be the ghostly lantern of a railroad worker killed by a runaway train. There are the "spooklights" of eastern Oklahoma and the eerie "will o' the wisps" of the bayou.

Most infamous of all perhaps is the dreaded "St. Elmo's Fire," a phenomenon reported by seafarers for centuries and thought to be the build-up of static electricity in a ship's rigging.

Catalina Island apparently had its own variation on these luminous phenomena in the form of what I call the "Backside Lights" as related to me by some well-known locals.

Several years ago, a group of kids and adults with the Avalon Day Camp was spending an overnight camping trip at Little Harbor. Sean Brannock, who was there overseeing the group, related how in the middle of the night an intense micro-burst of wind and rain hit the area. Most of the campers had no tents and were sleeping out on the ground when the weather hit.

"There we were in the middle of the night," said Sean, "everyone's sleeping and all of a sudden the wind starts to pick up."

The blasting wind was quickly joined by a sudden and dramatic downpour. "It POURED rain," he said, "like the hardest rain."

Lisa Keppel was there and was immediately concerned about what effect the deluge would have on the kids. "I said, 'Thank God these kids are sleeping'," she said.

As they lay there in their sleeping bags, staring into the night sky with nowhere to get out of the rain, they first noticed "them"—a number of strange, colored lights that were hovering in the sky above.

"There were all these flashing, different lights," said Sean. "They seemed like they were right above us, over our heads. They kept going on and off and changing to different colors...kind of like flashing, dancing lights."

Our local chef *extraordinaire* Greg Wenger was in the group, too. Unlike the others, he and his wife were inside a tent and it was the brightness of the objects that first woke him up. "The sky turned a bright orange like the sunset and you heard all kinds of weird noises, like giant fans going off," he said.

"We all got up and stared up at the sky with our mouths open."

"(The lights) were doing things like jumping up and down," he said, adding that there seemed to be no coordinated motion, but rather a chaotic pattern.

He described the lights as numbering from "about 15 to 18." Each one was spherical and about three-feet in diameter and they were all flying about 20 to 50 feet above the ground. While primarily a bright orange color ("like the color of fire"), he said they shifted through other colors as well "like a sunset."

It all ended somewhat abruptly when the rain and the wind stopped and the strange orbs simply vanished in the night.

"The thing about this was that none of us talked to each other that night," he said. It wasn't until the next morning that any of the stunned campers brought it up, said Greg. "We were at breakfast and it was like 20 people said they all saw the same thing and everyone's mouth was open. "

What could explain this bizarre phenomenon?

I exchanged emails with Dr. Robert Fovell, a specialist in "mesoscale meteorology" at UCLA. Evidently perplexed, Dr. Fovell said he had "no idea what was going on" and asked for more information.

I told him what I knew and brought up some of my own theories, including the possibility that this was an example of what's known as "ball lightning," an extremely rare and little understood weather phenomenon. With only a handful of reported cases in all of recorded history, "ball lightning" is thought to be a naturally-occurring electrical charge associated with thunderstorms that manifests itself in the form of glowing spheres that then proceed to wreak havoc.

Evidently none of my ideas impressed the good doctor, however. He simply replied "Unfortunately, I still have no clue. Sorry."

So, in the absence of any official explanation of the matter, I confess a bit of me is happy to report that the strange "Backside Lights" will go down in the books as yet another Catalina Island mystery.

WINDWARD WEIRDNESS

Catalina has long been a hotbed of UFO sightings going back even before the advent of the "Age of UFOs" beginning in the late 1940s. Just about anyone who's spent any amount of time in the Hills over the years will tell you they've seen "something" that they couldn't explain.

To skeptics, the sightings are generally chalked up to Catalina's proximity to regional military installations and the top secret programs in which those entities are involved. But believers in the extraterrestrial approach are legion and go back nearly a century.

As early as the 1920s, a group calling itself the Hollow Earth Society postulated that Catalina is one of several locations around the world that serves as a portal into a hypothesized "inner world" inhabited by an advanced civilization. The strange craft that people saw from time to time (the term "UFO" hadn't been invented yet) were nothing more than inhabitants of that nether world coming to the surface occasionally for a look-see.

Back in the early 1990s, Don Salvo was camping at Ben Weston beach. Isaac Felix happened to be there camping at the same time. Nothing unusual about that.

But on this particular occasion, sometime after midnight, they both noticed what appeared to be an unusual "craft" of some kind hovering low to the beach. Both Don and Isaac said it was too dark to make out any details about the craft, but that they could see it moving against the stars. Whatever it was, they said, was completely silent.

The craft then came to a stop while hovering above the beach and suddenly emitted three quick flashes of light. Once finished with that, the craft rapidly ascended out of view once again.

But the weirdness was only beginning. Don said that the next morning a US Marine Corps Sikorsky SH-1 Seahawk (the Navy's version of the legendary "Blackhawk") began flying around the beach.

Shortly after that, a civilian helicopter actually landed on the beach and out of it climbed several Japanese men in black suits and ties who then proceeded to look around the area. They didn't approach Don or Isaac, even though they were obviously aware of their presence. Instead, these "men in black" just inspected the beach area for a while before climbing back into the chopper and taking off.

Similar to this story is an account that former Islander Jim Lehr told me that happened to him at about roughly the same time frame, the 1990s. One morning about 3 a.m., Jim was up and about his condo at Sol Vista. From his living room he looked toward the back of Avalon Canyon and saw some kind of illuminated craft scoot over the ridge from the Palisades and then descend into the canyon.

He then watched with amazement as it drifted over the sleeping town of Avalon. As with Don and Isaac's sighting, Jim said the craft was completely silent—no sounds of any motor nor any whir of propellers.

Jim got on the phone and immediately called the Harbor Office on the pier, the only place he could think of where there would be someone on duty who was also in a position to be able to see what he had seen. Sure enough, one of the Harbor Patrol officers on duty had seen—and wondered about—the same thing.

At the risk of being unromantic, the most likely "earthly" explanation for both the Ben Weston sighting and Jim Lehr's Avalon Canyon sighting involves the then-emerging technology of drone aircraft or Unmanned Aerial Vehicles. These UAVs were just coming into their own in the early 1990s, such as the Sikorsky Cypher VTOL, possibly operated by the Navy out of San Clemente or San Nicolas Island.

Many of these UAVs use inducted fan propulsion systems, which are designed to render them virtually silent. The three flashes of light that Don saw would probably have been photographs being taken.

Although it's unsettling that the military might be using Catalina as a testing ground for their various contrivances (what else are they testing on us?), it's certainly not out of the question.

As far as the Marine Corps helicopter and the "Men in Black" are concerned, perhaps the Navy lost track of the UAV and, fearing it may have crashed on the Island, went out to look for it. The Japanese Men in Black may have been the "Tech Department" for a possible Japanese manufacturer, helping the Navy to look for their little lost prototype to see if they could get it flying again.

But then again, maybe what Don, Isaac and Jim saw was something else...

CATALINA'S STONEHENGE?

One of the earliest accounts of Catalina Island passed down through the centuries by early Spanish explorers tells us of a mysterious religious shrine belonging to the Island Tongva; a place that the Spaniards referred to as the "Temple of the Sun."

This temple was considered a central location for the worship of the Tongva deity Chinigchinich, which they considered to be the "sun god."

While the Chinigchinich religion was practiced by Tongva all over Southern California, Catalina is believed to be the cultural center of the religion and as such the Island has the lion's share of ceremonial artifacts and burial sites associated with it.

Now, before you go envisioning this temple as something out of "Raiders of the Lost Ark" with instant death traps and secret passages, you should know that it wasn't quite that extensive.

In fact, there seems to have been no actual structure per se, but rather an outdoor array of altars, ceremonial burial sites and large stones whose purpose has never been ascertained. Nevertheless, by some accounts the entire complex was as wide as two miles in diameter.

Since the temple is now gone, the only information we have to go on comes from the visit in 1602 of Spanish explorer Sebastian Vizcaino, the man who gave the Island the name "Santa Catalina." The only graphic representation of the site was a simple circle drawn by him on a map.

According to Vizcaino's chronicler, Father Torquemada, on the second day of their stopover at Catalina the Spaniards found "a level prairie, very well cleared, where the Indians were assembled to worship an idol which was there."

This idol, wrote Torquemada, "resembled a demon, having two horns, no head, a dog at its feet and many children painted all around it." The idol was also adorned with numerous eagle feathers, attached there by Tongva men from all over Southern California during annual rituals held at the site.

Upon seeing this "blasphemous" object, and against the warnings of the gathered Tongva, Vizcaino approached the idol and "made a cross and placed the name of Jesus on the head."

Within the circle near the idol were seen two large ravens. "The devil was in those crows (sic)," wrote Torquemada, "and spoke through them, for they were regarded with great respect and veneration."

Aware of this veneration for ravens, the Spanish soldiers did what we have come to expect from these men: they shot them both dead, an act which instantly brought "laments" from the Tongva, but didn't seem to adversely affect the rest of their stay at the Island.

What was the purpose of the Temple of the Sun? Was it purely of religious significance or did it have other uses as well?

Torquemada describes the center of the temple as being "formed by a large circle of long stones pointing upward toward the mid-day sun," in the center of which was the idol.

Given that the main purpose of the site was to worship the sun god, is it not conceivable that the stones were configured to record various astronomical events, such as the solstices and equinoxes? After all, they had to know when to hold their annual ceremony.

Unfortunately, we'll probably never know the answer to this, as the temple has long since disappeared, something we evidently can't blame on the zealous Spaniards. The site seems to have simply disappeared over the ensuing centuries, possibly due to intense rains.

Even our controversial artifact hunter from the 1920s, Ralph Glidden, didn't venture a guess other than to possibly attribute its disappearance to earthquakes or landslides.

Although the site was believed to be either in the actual cradle of the Isthmus or perhaps on the plateau above the east side of Two Harbors near the buffalo pens, no trace of it has ever been found.

LAND OF THE GIANTS

Throughout the history of North America, tales abound of the discovery of the remains of abnormally large and even "giant" pre-historic humans.

While archaeologists shrug off such claims as pure fiction, Photoshop jobs, or perhaps the natural elongation of normal human skeletons as they settle over the course of centuries, this phenomenon has developed its own little cottage industry within the realm of paranormal researchers.

In 1895, a burial mound containing 20 skeletons "twice as large as those of present-day people" was discovered near Toledo, Ohio. The skeletons were reportedly all arranged in a sitting position and facing east.

In 1931, a number of large skeletons were discovered in a lake bed near Lovelock, Nevada, one of which was said to be almost 10–feet long. Another specimen measuring 8 ½-feet in length was also discovered and appeared to be wrapped in a "gum-covered" fabric similar to Egyptian mummies.

In 1965, a skeleton measuring 8-feet nine-inches in length was reportedly discovered in Holly Creek, Kentucky, with a skull "30 inches in circumference."

As you might have guessed by now, Catalina Island counts itself as one of the locations of these finds. Not so long ago in our history there was a fellow by the name of Ralph Glidden who took it upon himself to excavate (some would say "plunder") the various Native American middens and burial sites around the Island.

In the days before the science of archaeology was born, men like Glidden did little more than exploit the artifacts and even the remains of Native Americans as a sort of lucrative "hobby." He ghoulishly displayed many of these remains and even offered them up for sale in a small "museum" he operated on Hill Street on Avalon's west side.

Among Glidden's many claims was that he had discovered the skeletal remains of 7-foot to 8-foot tall "giants" in various places around the Island.

The question of just what the giants were up to is as fascinating as their discovery itself. The answer to that question, I am told, has to do with what is known as the Hollow Earth theory, or the belief that within the earth is a vast open realm inhabited by an advanced civilization.

While the Hollow Earth theory enjoyed its heydey back in the 19th century and early 20th century, it still has a number of followers.

The Russian newspaper *Pravda*, for example, regularly features bonafied "scientific" articles on the existence of this global under-realm. As recently as June 6, 2011, that esteemed journal published an article titled "Parallel World Hidden Inside Earth" and in 2007 featured a similar article entitled "Another Human Civilization May Live Inside Earth's Hollows."

While the articles themselves don't offer any proof of these claims (ahem), the authors pull no punches in espousing their own beliefs on this notion, quoting various "researchers" in the bargain.

Enter Catalina Island: Although "Hollow Earthers" believe that the major entry points into this underworld are located at the earth's north and south poles, they claim there are numerous alternate portals (emergency exits?) located around the world, including—you guessed it—Catalina Island.

As a matter of fact, back in the 1920s a contingent from the Hollow Earth Society made a special trip out to Catalina in an effort to search for just such a portal. No word on whether or not they found anything.

It is said that these giants, including those supposedly found on Catalina, were given the task of protecting these portals. In other words, they were thought to be the "guardians" of the portals into this underworld, protecting this internal civilization from incursions from above.

The specter of the existence of such a portal on the Island makes a perfect segue into our next segment, about a mysterious door that appears from time to time in the hills of Catalina...

THE GREEN DOOR

From the mysterious environs of the beautiful, secluded cove known as Toyon Bay come a number of Catalina Island's mysteries. One of the most bizarre revolves around sightings of what is quite simply known as "The Green Door."

Reported by various Toyon Bay residents and visitors over the years, the Green Door is, literally, a bright green door that mysterious appears (and subsequently disappears) in the tributary canyons of Toyon. Hikers in the canyons sometimes report seeing the door flush against a canyon wall or even floating in mid-air. Sometimes the door is open, other times it is closed.

Carolyn Price and three of her friends came across the infamous portal during a hike one day in 1974. "It was maybe four feet up and flush with the hill and the chaparral," she said, "as though it had always been there—I had just never seen it."

Carolyn described the color as a bright, natural green "like the grass on the hills of Catalina in the springtime." The sides were paneled and the shape was rectangular except for a rounded top, she said.

Curiosity led her and her friends closer to the object, but something else was drawing them in, too. "There was a force, an energy—visceral—pulling us towards it. I felt as if we were being taken to it; that we could do no other."

One of her fellow hikers did what you're never supposed to do in the old horror films: she opened the door...

"It was dark inside, really dark," said Carolyn, "and seemed to go on forever."

At this point, Carolyn remembered thinking that the force was going to suck her friend inside "and take her away." It was then that her friend screamed and the four of them "hauled our teenage selves as far and quickly away from that place as we could."

No sign of the Green Door was found in subsequent searches, although it has reportedly shown up—and later vanished—in other nearby areas over the years.

But should you, Dear Reader, someday find—and gather the courage to open—the Green Door, would you go inside? Given the nature of some of the area's other paranormal stories, it appears that maybe others have.

Such a possible connection with The Green Door can be found in the disturbing story of the "little red-haired girl."

The story goes that, shortly after World War II, when the camp was opened up again to private interests after its war-time occupation by the Office of Strategic Services, a little girl (red-haired, of course) and her brother went out playing in the nearby canyons one day. The little girl and her brother never returned home and the legend says that all efforts to find them ended in failure.

The boy was never seen again, but residents of Toyon Bay over the years have reported seeing the spiritual incarnation of the little girl from time to time.

In one cottage in particular in the multi-building complex that makes up the Catalina Island Marine Institute at Toyon Bay, residents will hear footsteps leading up to one of the rooms, followed by a knock on the door. Upon opening the door, there is the little girl in all her red-haired glory, staring forlornly and silently at the startled occupant. After a few moments, the girl simply vanishes into thin air.

Carolyn remembered seeing the girl one day while walking through the complex of cottages and buildings. The sighting was in broad daylight and the girl was actually beckoning Carolyn to come with her. The little girl wordlessly led her to the cottage of one of Carolyn's friends, a young man who was, it just so happens, was lonely at the time and wanted to talk to Carolyn. How the little girl knew this only adds to the mystery.

Did the little girl and her brother enter the Green Door and vanish into some alternate dimension, only to be allowed out now and then to scare the proverbial pants off the living?. Will she ever be "returned" permanently to her native realm? Or is she destined to be stuck forever at her young age in some unknown dimension?

Is the Green Door one of the portals to the Hollow Earth as outlined in the preceding segment on "Land of the Giants"? Or could there be another candidate for one of these portals on Catalina? You may want to read the segment "The Most Mysterious Mine of All" in the chapter "Lost & Forgotten" in this book for more insight.

A MOST EXTRAORDINARY GENTLEMAN

Next Halloween, if you're a little too old for trick-or-treating but still enjoy a little "out of this world" diversion now and then, take a stroll up Cemetery Road in Avalon and pay a visit to a dear departed individual who is quite possibly—as Yogi Berra might say—the most famous resident of Avalon Cemetery that no one ever heard of.

Beyond the cemetery's arching wrought-iron gates, tucked away in the park's southeast corner you will find the very ordinary grave of a very extraordinary man. Here lies the body of physicist, inventor, man of mystery, devoted father and beloved husband Thomas Townsend Brown.

While Albert Einstein was a theorist who postulated the impossible on paper, Brown was the tinkerer who spent a lifetime trying to bring such theories to life.

And while his most well-known invention was the ionic air purifier, the true story of his genius can be found not in this somewhat mundane household appliance, but rather in the science and experimentation that lead to and surpassed its development.

The ionic air purifier—actually the result of an effort to make a wireless, woofer-less audio speaker—was not much more than an economically viable by-product of Brown's pursuit to unlock the inter-dimensional secrets of the universe and the elusive, symbiotic relationship between electromagnetism and gravity.

This 60-year pursuit, which included the discovery of the Brown-Bayfield effect, took him on an Indiana Jones/James Bond adventure from the Roaring '20s to the rise and fall of the Third Reich, the

UFO phenomena of the 1950s and through the spectacular discoveries in quantum physics in the 1960s and '70s.

He was rumored to be one of the key players in the infamous "Philadelphia Experiment," a role he refused to talk about until his dying day.

His later years saw him involved in the sudden emergence of UFO sightings on the world scene and even in the space race itself and finally to his last years on Catalina, where he continued his experiments on the Island that considered "very special" for its various quantum properties.

The mysterious life of Townsend Brown spanned a mercurial era in world history that was perfectly fitted to men of his intelligence and imagination. Historians, UFO experts and general conspiracy theorists will debate the significance of his accomplishments forever.

But in all probability, the truth about the life and times of Brown will never be known. The details will remain forever locked away in that very ordinary grave in the southeast corner of the Avalon Cemetery.

A QUANTUM LEAP

At the core of Townsend Brown's scientific beliefs was his personal Holy Grail of somehow unifying electromagnetism and gravity, an idea he outlined in his August 1929 article in *Science & Technology* magazine entitled "How I Control Gravitation."

This ability to reconcile these two forces of nature—if successfully accomplished in the laboratory and then on the assembly line—would mean human flight without the encumbrance of gravity nor the hazards and inconvenience of fossil fuels.

In fact, at one point in his career, his pursuit of anti-gravitational flight was in part aimed at explaining the scientific possibility of flying saucers; a pursuit that exposed him to a certain amount of criticism, which he was never truly able to shake.

In the 1920s, at about the same time Brown was formulating his theories about the physical nature of the universe, the scientific discipline known as "quantum physics" was beginning to gain traction in an increasingly technological world.

Although quantum physics can be traced back to Newtonian times, this relatively new branch of physics was aimed at science on an atomic and molecular level and represented for the first time since the advent of empirical science a willingness on the part of physicists to accept the idea that answers to some of science's most pressing questions might be found not within our three dimensional universe, but rather in realms that included higher, as yet undiscovered dimensions.

For example, after centuries of human philosophy, religion, art and science, we humans still don't really know what "causes" gravity. It is such an integral part of our lives that we don't give it any more thought than we do the air we breathe.

Like breathing, only when someone brings it up in conversation do we even give it a thought.

And yet science still can't explain what it is.

We know why the sky is blue and why grass is green. We know what pi is to the billionth decimal (and beyond) and we know what causes malaria and why birds sing the songs they sing. We know exactly what phase the moon will be in a thousand years from today, but we still don't know why a pencil falls straight to the floor when let go.

Physicists have somewhat reluctantly come to the conclusion that our three-dimensional universe simply cannot provide us with a concrete reason for why an immense mass such as a planet or a star can attract other massive objects.

It was the revolutionary concepts of quantum mechanics that spurred Brown into postulating that effects that are commonly observed in day-to-day life in our three-dimensional universe might very well be the result of actions occurring in a not-so-theoretical fourth spatial dimension.

"My dad was invested with what I call some sort of 'mental download ability,'" said Linda Leach, Brown's daughter. Rather than scaling a mountain of information to get to the answer at the top, Linda said, people with this ability "wake up in the morning and already know something and then spend the next six months trying to explain it to people."

THE PHILADELPHIA EXPERIMENT

In 1930, Brown began applying his talents and knowledge toward military research with his enlistment in the U.S. Navy, a love-hate relationship that lasted nearly to the end of World War II.

Like most of his life, his role during the war is somewhat obscure, but it appears that his most celebrated brush with the nebulous world of the quantum unknown was his clandestine role in the so-called Philadelphia Experiment in which the Navy purportedly attempted to render an entire ship "invisible" to human eyes.

Skeptics claim there never was any such experiment, while believers—such as Charles Berlitz—offer a bewildering array of "facts" and "personal accounts" of the event.

In fact, it's not even known whether Brown played a role at all in the experiment, although Catalina residents who quizzed him about this from time to time state that he did not deny any role. He simply wouldn't talk about it.

One thing is certain: if indeed the Navy attempted an experiment of any sort using radiation and quantum physics, Thomas Townsend Brown would have been the man they would have chosen to head the project. He was already working for them and his expertise in these matters was virtually unparalleled.

The purpose behind the experiment was to develop a "cloaking device" using technology largely developed by Brown and his fellow researchers that was capable of rendering a ship—in this case the destroyer U.S.S. Elwood—invisible to enemy eyes.

According to some accounts, a number of sailors died during the experiment or disappeared as a result of the experiment gone awry. Popular accounts claim that some of the missing sailors were never found and others say that a number of them "woke up" weeks after the experiment finding themselves hundreds or thousands of miles away.

But the Philadelphia Experiment was only one of the events that helped to develop an aura of mystery around Brown. As Brown would learn in the post-war years, another quick way to attract attention from his critics was to delve into the world of "flying saucers."

UFOs

In the late 1940s, the world experienced a flurry of sightings of strange flying craft or "UFOs" and the idea that these airborne vehicles were alien spacecraft visiting earth was not considered at all far-fetched. After all, the world had just experienced a global world war, the likes of which had never been seen before. The weapons and the technology that had been developed (and used) were inconceivable only a few short years before.

In the space of a few short years fighter aircraft had evolved from largely fabric-covered, propeller-driven bi-planes to aluminum-sheathed "jets" and the weapons they delivered transformed from low-caliber machine guns to highly-accurate and lightweight missiles and bombs, including that well-known device that could destroy entire cities.

The term "flying saucer" was first coined in the late 1940s after the famous Roswell, New Mexico, incident in which the purported debris of a "flying disk" was reported by the U.S. Army and the *Roswell Daily Record*. The story was quickly altered by the Army Air Force in the days following the "crash," claiming that the debris was actually the result of the crash of a top secret weather balloon.

Whether or not the Army's new account of the incident was credible or not mattered little. The "bell had been rung" and an entire sub-culture was created around the idea that the "flying saucer" was indeed of extraterrestrial origin.

In the mid-1950s, Brown himself became an investigator of the new UFO phenomenon, which he felt went hand-in-hand with his pioneering research into anti-gravity. He founded NICAP, the National Investigations Committee on Aerial Phenomena in 1956, an organization that still exists today.

"He didn't start NICAP to prove that UFOs existed," said his daughter. "He already knew they existed."

As a child, Linda often helped her father with his fascinating work load, which often meant sifting through enormous stacks of UFO reports gathered from scientists around the world. "Look for one that wobbles," he would tell his daughter as she sifted through the reports. "Look for reports where the saucer was reported to be wobbling." He was "on to their propulsion," she said.

"I asked him 'why don't they land on the White House lawn,'" she said. "They don't have to," he would tell her. "They already know everything they need to know." Such a high profile meeting, he would tell her, would be "bad for both parties involved."

THE CATALINA YEARS

After many decades of moving from city to city and even country to country, Brown made the decision in 1971 to move his family from San Francisco to Catalina Island. Although he had visited the Island on at least two occasions as a child, he viewed the Island in an entirely different light in his later years.

"He came to the Island on a Friday and looked around and liked it," said Linda.

She said her father immediately contacted Joe Guion, who operated not only a boat rental business on the Island, but handled real estate as well.

According to Linda, within three days Brown had rented not only the historic old Wolf house on Chimes Tower Road where the family would initially live, but he had also rented office space in the now-Catalina Conservancy headquarters at 3rd and Clarissa streets and a building at Bird Park to use as his laboratory. (Eventually the family moved in to one of the old Quonset huts at Pebbly Beach, where he ultimately did most of his research).

Linda said that there were a number of reasons why her father liked Catalina other than the Island's beauty. "He liked Catalina because it was isolated," she said, adding that this isolation meant less interference for his research projects.

In addition, he felt that the Island's geology had special and unique properties well suited to his research. This research, according to Linda, revolved around rocks. Plain, ordinary rocks—at least to the untrained eye.

"I worked for him taking readings from his recorders," she said. "The recorders were constantly running. I would take a reading about every half an hour."

And just what were the recorders recording? "Sidereal radiation," she said, referring to a still-controversial subject in physics.

It was this "sidereal radiation," it seems, that gave Brown's carefully chosen collection of rocks—rocks from around the world—

a slight electrical charge. According to Linda, her father would scour the rocks along the shore at Pebbly Beach until he found "just the right one." He would then hook up negative and positive terminals to it and a slight electrical charge would register.

Linda recalled an incident in the late 1970s in which four crew members of a U.S. Navy nuclear submarine visited the Brown's Quonset hut at Pebbly Beach. The crew members, which included one officer, picked up an "apparatus" consisting of a number of Brown's special stones gleaned from the shores of Catalina over the years by Brown.

Linda said the crew then left the Brown home. The submarine sailed away a short time later leaving Linda to speculate about the episode. "I've always wondered what that was about."

Linda theorizes that another reason for the Brown family's hasty jump from the Bay Area to Catalina may have involved the controversial discipline of "remote viewing," wherein participants are trained to psychically "see" a distant location as part of a psychic or perhaps out-of-body experience. Linda knew that her father had been involved with a remote viewing research at Stanford University in the late 1960s.

Such research had possibly taken place on the Island before. It is believed that during World War II, the Office of Strategic Services, or OSS (the precursor to today's CIA) conducted remote viewing experimentation at their facility at Toyon Bay, two miles north of Avalon.

Given the nature of Brown's work, it was only natural for him to wax philosophic about life. One conversation Linda remembers involved the nature of Time. "I got into a discussion with him about how Time travels in a straight line, one thing happening after another."

"No, sweetie," he told her, arguing for the non-linear approach. "Time is more like the ocean," he said. "The waves come in and go back out.'"

While he had his ideas on the physical nature of the universe, he was less expressive on the subject of the immortal soul. "He had a very strong feeling that there was a Creator," she said, adding that her father was not a church attendee. "He never spoke of Heaven or Hell and he didn't buy into darkness and evil. He just basically said that there is no darkness that can fight light.

"Wherever there is light," he would tell her, "the darkness has to go away. To give any more power to darkness was foolish."

The day was drawing closer, Brown knew, when he would inevitably learn about the immortal—or perhaps mortal—nature of the soul. One day, with his daughter on hand, he chose his final resting spot in the southeast corner of Avalon Cemetery.

"I was with him when he picked the spot," said Linda. "He wanted it to be near the bench because he wanted people who visited him to have a place to rest and be comfortable. That's just the way he was."

Brown died in his sleep, "like when a child takes a nap." "He was exactly where he wanted to be, on Catalina," she said, noting that after a lifetime of moving around, only Catalina had managed to find its way into her father's heart as a place to genuinely call home.

"He always loved the people of Catalina," she said.

A love of animals pervaded Brown's life ("He never considered an animal less than a human") and often provided fodder for philosophical analogies. In one case, this resulted in the comparison of puppies to the members of the human race, poised on the brink of great discoveries: "Puppies never really get up and walk around very much," he told her, "until the day they open their eyes."

"We are just like these puppies," he said. "Our eyes are closed."

"But when we finally open them, watch out."

Lost & Forgotten

LOST TREASURE &
FORGOTTEN MINES

The waters around Catalina are the final resting place for scores of ships, some of which went down with fortunes that have yet to be found. Likewise, the canyons of Catalina are riddled with natural caverns and long-lost mines, legacies of a violent volcanic past and a once thriving mining history.

THE FATEFUL VOYAGE OF THE *SAN SEBASTIAN*

It's a cold, clear day on the open sea and with the wind mercifully behind her, the Spanish galleon *San Sebastian* leaps across the deep ocean swells.

But in hot pursuit of the *Sebastian* is another sailing vessel, this one a corsair filled with a gallery of rogues under the command of English pirate George Compton. Like his contemporaries Sir Francis Drake and Sir Thomas Cavendish, Compton terrorized Spanish shipping in the Pacific waters of North America a century before the world would hear the names Blackbeard or Captain Kidd.

But the *San Sebastian* cannot move through the water with nearly the swiftness of the pursuing corsair. Like all galleons, she was built for brawn and not for speed. She was designed not to win races, but to redistribute the world's wealth in favor of Europe's distant royalty. She is literally loaded to the gunnels with tons of sparkling treasures from the Far East and it is the goal of Compton and his men to relieve her of this burden.

The captain and crew of the *Sebastian* are a long way from help and home—a home they justifiably fear never setting eyes on again. They know they have only one chance and it's not a particularly appealing one at that.

"Head her into the island!," yells the *capitan* to his astonished helmsman. "Drive her ashore!"

The sudden report of a bow cannon from the English ship shrieks across the waves, startling the crew of the *Sebastian* and driving deeper into their souls their immediate peril.

The lead ball screams past the galleon's mizzen mast and plunges violently into the sea off the *Sebastian*'s starboard beam. On the corsair, the predators let out a terrible cheer that sounds like the barking of wild hounds.

As the deep waters turn to turquoise shallows and shoals, a lookout on the bow of the *Sebastian* reports the first sighting of undersea rocks and kelp. The island is getting closer.

Suddenly, the merchant ship jolts and then shudders violently, tossing sailors to the deck and causing the ship's loose rigging to crack like a thousand bullwhips.

"*Váyanse, hombres! Corren para la vida!,*" yells the captain. "Go! Run for your lives!"

With that, the terrified crew scrambles into the launches and over the rails. Untrained in the exotic sport of swimming, many flounder in the water and drown right there in six feet of salt water.

Those who survive the exodus hurry onto the shores of the unknown island where they might find deliverance in the scrub-oak hills and jungles.

Crewless now, the *Sebastian*'s sails are back-winded and she is once again drawn to seaward by the same winds that drove her ashore. Now in deeper waters, her savaged hull gulps seawater by the barrel until she heals to starboard and sinks forever into the blue, taking her fortune with her.

Enraged at losing their pay for a morning's hard work, Compton and his crew fan out into the Island's desolate canyons to find all of the *Sebastian*'s crewmembers. The hapless Spaniards are all caught and hauled back to the beach where they are brutally beaten, shot and God-knows-what-else until, to a man, they are dead.

This is not a scene played out in the latest Johnny Depp film or the climactic battle scene of an Errol Flynn movie. Nor is it an event that took place in some far-flung tropic isle in the Caribbean or South China Sea.

It's a real-life event that happened on the West End of Catalina Island.

In fact, it occurred on the morning of January 7, 1754, and whether the souls of the unfortunate Spanish mariners have found peace or are even now wandering the silent empty canyons of the West End is uncertain.

But one thing is certain: the vast treasure that was both their duty and their demise is still buried somewhere deep in the shifting sands off Catalina.

In fact, since the wreck of the San Sebastian is located less than a couple of football fields off Catalina's backside, it's possible that some fisherman, yachtsman or kayaker is even now gliding their watercraft directly above her treasure; a treasure that would likely be worth tens of millions, if not hundreds of millions of dollars these days.

To date, no one is known to have ever looked for the wreck of the *Sebastian*. Despite the seemingly concise distance of "170 feet" offshore, without knowing exactly where she sank it still leaves a lot of ground to cover.

It's entirely possible, however, that with future advances in remote sensing technology, that the wealth to be gained by such a find may finally spur someone into launching a treasure hunt for her.

THE WRECK OF THE *SAN PEDRO*

For those of us returning to the Island after our mainland Costco trips and doctor appointments, the sight of Catalina rising out of the channel is a welcome one.

But to many a mariner over the centuries, the bold cliffs and high peaks rising from the deep Pacific waters has held terror and dread, not hearth and home.

Mariners from the age of Renaissance Europe understandably viewed the windswept Channel Islands of California as foreboding and perilous places, lonely and detached from the warm cobblestone streets of their homes in Toledo and Cadiz. To many a mariner, they spelled disaster.

Such an unfortunate lot was the crew of the Spanish merchant ship *San Pedro*. In 1598, or possibly 1600, the *San Pedro* found herself floundering in the lee of Catalina's West End after enduring a brutal trans-Pacific crossing from the Philippines.

Battered by storms and the incessant Northwesterlies, the ship rounded the West End and turned towards Arrow Point. At that point the hapless merchantman either completely fell to pieces or crashed straight into the rocks and then sank. One way or the other, it spelled doom for the ship.

The lives of all hands were apparently spared and the crew later made its way back safely to New Spain, the country we now call Mexico.

But the ship was lost along with her enormously valuable cargo of gold, silver, silks, ivory and more; doubtless scattered through her breached hull along the steeply sloped submarine shore.

But the story of the *San Pedro* doesn't end there. In fact, it's only the beginning...

Perhaps I should have titled this segment "The Wreck AND SALVAGE of the *San Pedro*." For unlike the majority of shipwrecks in the annals of maritime history, the fascinating story of the San Pedro was to continue long after her unfortunate encounter with Arrow Point.

The modern story begins in the early 1970s with the entrance of one Charles A. Kenworthy, a wealthy Southern California real estate mogul and part-time treasure hunter. It was said that Kenworthy spared no expense in the procurement of any and all documents related to the possible whereabouts of lost treasure, whether on land or sea.

Kenworthy was going to search for the *San Pedro* and, to his credit, he jumped through all of the hoops necessary to gain approval and permits from the State of California. In July of 1974, an exploratory permit was issued allowing Kenworthy to search for— but not salvage (not just yet anyway)—the long-lost *San Pedro*.

Kenworthy even sought—and by some accounts received— support from none other than John Wayne, going so far as to try to enlist the support of Wayne's vessel the *Wild Goose*, a common sight in Catalina waters in those days.

But problems were just on the horizon for Kenworthy. Just as he was setting up his operation, another ship appeared on the scene in the form of none other than Howard Hughes' research ship the famed *Glomar Explorer*. The crew of the *Glomar Explorer* proceeded to cordon off the area surrounding their ship in a diameter of nearly half a mile and began their operations.

Dave Hood, a former crew member on a SCUBA charter boat operating out of Two Harbors recounts on the official Hughes *Glomar Explorer* Facebook page an incident in the Spring of 1974 when his boat got a little too close to the "research" vessel.

Hood had heard the vessel was "searching for a sunken treasure ship," a rumor that was reinforced when his vessel was chased away from the scene by guards from the *Glomar Explorer* brandishing Smith & Wesson M76 submachine guns. All of this activity led Kenworthy to believe, quite understandably, that the *Glomar Explorer* was there to hog in on his treasure-hunting operation.

But here is where the plot thickens. Recently declassified government documents and a fascinating documentary by Director Michael White called *Azorian: the Raising of the K-129* bring a whole new twist to the story, arguing that the *Glomar Explorer* was not, in fact, looking for traditional buried treasure. Rather, the ship was preparing for a highly clandestine mission to recover a less traditional form of treasure: military secrets from a sunken Soviet submarine thousands of miles away in the North Pacific.

At midnight on March 11, 1968, nuclear-armed Soviet submarine K-129 suffered a series of catastrophic explosions that sent her and her crew to the bottom of the Pacific 800 miles north of Hawaii in about 15,000 feet of water. At those depths, the entire crew no doubt died instantly and, lacking the technology to determine her exact position, the Russians had to give her up for lost.

The U.S. Navy, however, *did* have the technology to not only detect the initial blasts themselves but the location of where the sub went down. In the Cold War world, the potential for the recovery of highly classified Soviet intelligence and technology was too tempting and Herculean efforts began to attempt a retrieval of the sunken sub.

In order to not raise the suspicions of the highly protective Soviet Navy, the CIA had to come up with a cover story as to just exactly why they were poking around in the area where the sub sank. The plan was to disguise their covert maritime activities as an expedition to mine the rich deposits of manganese littering the ocean floor around the Soviet wreck.

This is where Hughes came in. Hughes was enlisted by the CIA to essentially "pretend" that he was building the *Glomar Explorer* for this purpose, since it would have looked suspicious for a non-commercial entity—the CIA in particular—to do so.

So, under the funding and direction of the CIA, Hughes' corporation embarked on a three-year mission to build the colossal 619-foot-long *Glomar Explorer*. Within the hold of the *Explorer* was a smaller, but still gargantuan, retrieval device nicknamed "Clementine" that would actually descend to the ocean floor, grab the sub, and hopefully return it to the mother ship at the surface.

Since "Clementine" and the *Glomar Explorer* were being constructed in two different areas, a rendezvous point had to be chosen where the two would be paired up before setting out to grab the Russian sub. The West End of Catalina Island was the perfect choice, not only because the waters surrounding the Island were shallow enough to allow for the operation, but because the Island was far enough from the mainland to be out of view of the general public, yet reasonably close to the two ports where the separate vessels would be launched—Long Beach and Redwood City in San Francisco Bay.

The remainder of the story of the *Glomar Explorer* and its attempts to retrieve the Soviet sub could fill another book, but it has little or nothing to do with Catalina, so I won't go into that other than to say the operation was mostly successful and the CIA came away with enough of the Soviet sub to keep them happy for a while.

But the real question is: Was it just a coincidence that the area also happened to be in the same location as the *San Pedro* and all her alleged millions in treasure? Howard Hughes was no dummy and he may very well have made it a condition of his agreement with the government that—in exchange for the right to use his name in their cover story—he be allowed to work the old Spanish shipwreck. After all, they were in the neighborhood.

In a Facebook posting on March 8, 2010, by a user known as "gollum," it is claimed that years after the incident, Kenworthy met up with some former *Glomar Explorer* crew members who admitted that, yes, they did in fact recover "much of the wreck and the gold and silver."

For Hughes, it would have been a perfect government-certified cover story within a government-certified cover story. Making millions not only off the U.S. government, but by working a Spanish shipwreck as well.

But our story still doesn't end there. Fast forward now to 1979 when marine archaeologist Jim Muche and his then-girlfriend (later wife) Lani began what was most likely the last official attempt to salvage the wreck of the *San Pedro*.

Although Muche didn't have the same level of technology at his disposal, his operation was far less costly than that of Kenworthy. After filing for, and obtaining, the necessary permits (such as the then-fledgling Environmental Impact Report), Jim and Lani spent the summer of 1979 diving the cool deep waters around Arrow Point in search of fortune, if not fame.

After a goodly amount of research on the internet, I managed to track Jim and Lani Muche down. They are both active nowadays in the world of both vintage World War II aircraft and equestrian interests as well.

I had one simple, obvious question for them: "Did you find anything?" Considering the pricey lifestyle revolving around warbirds and thoroughbreds one might assume the answer would be "yes." But that would be pure speculation on my part, because...

Unfortunately, my calls were never returned and my emails never answered.

Perhaps one day I will receive a reply and the shifting submarine sands of Arrow Point will shed just a little more light on the mystery of the wreck of the *San Pedro*.

CATALINA'S "UNDERWORLD"

We all know and love the fresh air and rolling green hills of Catalina in the springtime; hills that fade to khaki beneath Monet skies in the summer. But few people are aware that beneath this splendor the Island is riddled with natural caves and the long-lost tunnels and forgotten mines of a bygone era when a significant portion of the Island's revenue was gained by mineral operations.

The earth's "underworld" has always held a fascination for us surface-dwelling critters as represented by the venerable Jules Verne classic *Journey to the Centre of the Earth*, which was made into one of those Saturday matinee-type films I grew up on. (The very name of this book, in fact, was inspired by Verne's *L'île Mysterieuse*, or "The Mysterious Island").

While most natural caves on Catalina are of relatively shallow depth, that is not the case with many of her mines.

The Blackjack Mine, for example, was an awesome labyrinth of tunnels extending thousands of feet into the nearby hillside. Although the mine (which was used in the 1920s for the extraction of a conglomerate of silver, lead and zinc known as "galena") has been idle now for many decades, the tunnels still exist down there, silent now to the sounds of toil and labor and the clang of metal on stone.

CAVES

The most visible cave on the Island is the one just below the Holly Hill House near the Cabrillo Mole. New visitors to the Island are often seen here, happily snapping digital photos of this, their first discovery on an enchanted isle. While this is not a natural cave, its origins are nonetheless fascinating.

Back in the 1890s when the founders of the newly-formed town of Avalon wanted to build a road out to Pebbly Beach, they ran into an obstacle by the name of Peter Gano. Gano, the owner and builder of what is now called the Holly Hill House, also owned part of the land through which the road was to be built.

Gano wouldn't allow the town access to his property, so—rather than build the road along the shore—it was decided to literally blast a tunnel through the mountain. The idea was not so much to actually drive the tunnel through the hill, but to annoy Gano so much with the day-to-day blasts of dynamite that he would give in—which he eventually did. Today, this shallow cave is the legacy of this old-time feud.

The majority of the Island's most fascinating natural caves are found on the Island's West End and, to a lesser extent, along the lee shore leading there. SCUBA divers, snorkelers and kayakers visiting Two Harbors regularly enjoy the complex of caves that includes Blue Cavern and Perdition Cave along with a Swiss cheese-platter of smaller caves—both wet and dry—that riddle the headlands around the Isthmus.

Blue Cavern is possibly our most famous cave. It's large enough to accommodate a number of inflatables as well as sea kayaks. One section of the cave, battered out by eons of Nor'easters, continues through the rock where it exits several yards away from the main entrance. This offshoot is large enough to navigate using kayaks or inflatables, affording adventurers their own abbreviated "Pirates of the Caribbean" adventure in the wild.

About midway between the Isthmus and Avalon is a wet cave, whose name escapes me at the moment, with a narrow entrance just large enough for a single inflatable. Once inside, the cave opens up into a larger chamber. From this "foyer" one can decide to continue on foot, scrabbling over cantaloupe-sized rocks constantly awash in the tidal surge, to a secluded subterranean beach of fine sand.

At Long Point is another well-known cave. This one pierces the headland allowing one to see all the way through the mountain to blue sky. When properly aligned from the sea, the tunnel takes on the shape (sort of) of Catalina Island.

On the backside of the Island, beneath Ribbon Rock, is another deep submarine cave. I remember once while paddling my kayak around the Island bumping into some commercial lobster fishermen who were exploiting the bugs down there. They had a long air hose disappearing into the cavern connected to a diver, while his fellow bug hunter drifted along in a skiff outside the cave with the compressor aboard.

We exchanged the typical maritime courtesies and I was rewarded with a large lobster that I cooked over my campfire that night at Little Harbor.

But some natural caves are more elusive and have defied exploration over the years. When I reached my 40th birthday several (ahem) years ago, rather than the traditional beer bash and cake and stuff, I opted instead to pass this milestone by paddling on a multi-day kayak trip along the Island's lee shore.

At one point, I pulled my kayak up on shore for a little rest when I noticed a small, dark opening between the sandy beach and an ancient lava flow. The entrance was nearly covered by fine beach sand, but I was able to shine my flashlight down inside, revealing a sandy floor several feet below.

Using my forearms, I shoveled enough sand out of the way to make myself a nice little entry point, about two-feet wide by a foot high. With flashlight in hand, I then slid head first down into the hole.

Once inside, I surveyed my new surroundings. The cave was not large, but was of comfortable size, about that of a typical Avalon living room. The ceiling was about a foot or two above my head and I noticed there seemed to be no ventilation or "sighing" sounds, indicating that the only opening to the cave was the one through which I had entered.

The floor was completely flat, compact sand, leading me to believe it was at times filled with either rainy season flood waters, extreme high-tide seawater, or waves from the occasional Nor'easter.

There were two things of interest in the cave. Along one side was the bleached skeleton of what must have been an enormous wild pig. To the right of that was a pair of ancient water cans, the old square tin variety, both of which were rusted out at the bottom, but otherwise fairly well preserved.

I had a vague feeling of unease being in there and thoughts of Hantavirus and scenes from *Lord of the Flies* whirled through my mind. It was not, I decided, the kind of place I would want to spend much time unless there was nowhere else to go.

Recently, I made a trip back to the same spot with Avalon's outboard repair guru Jim Parrish to see if I could once again locate

"Pig Sty Cave" as I had named it. But look as we might, we weren't able to find it.

The place where I recall finding it was instead covered with masses of beach rock. No doubt in the intervening decade, Santa Ana storms and assorted wave actions must have buried the entrance. For all I know, I may have made my initial discovery during a brief window of time over the past century when the entrance was accessible.

Disappointed, Jim and I headed back to Avalon. The Island doesn't give up her secrets easily.

MINES

For nearly a century, Catalina Island was poked and prodded by mining interests in the pursuit of a variety of earth's metallic treasures, notably silver, lead and zinc and (to a far lesser extent) gold. The remnants of this once robust era are still out there in the hills and there is no shortage of mystery surrounding them.

For obvious reasons I won't divulge the exact locations of any of these mines. Nothing will make you the subject of a future *Mysterious Island* chapter faster than to disappear forever into one of these holes. In addition, most of them are on private property whose owners don't take kindly to such trespasses. In any case, most of them have been sealed up and are flooded with ground water.

There is an old legend about the first discovery of gold on the Island that has been haunting Catalina history books for more than a century. In 1832, a man named George C. Yount was on a seal otter hunt along the leeward coast of Catalina. During one of his visits to shore he claims he came across a "ledge of gold-bearing quartz." He grabbed himself a chunk of the material (which he later claims he lost), but for some reason wasn't impressed enough at the time to look for more.

Over the ensuing 20 years, Yount returned to the Island three times to try to find this lode once again, but to no avail. The tales of his purported discovery, however, propelled Catalina Island into the world of large-scale mining—an episode that lasted nearly a century.

The true mining history of Catalina doesn't so much start with Yount's discovery, but with our own mini-Gold Rush in the Civil War era; an interesting interlude in Catalina's history complete with its own gold rush town called "Queen City" at the Island's West End. The "rush" didn't last for long, however, due mostly to the fact that no one was finding any gold along with the fact that the Union Army decided to evict all the miners so they could set up their operations at the Isthmus.

In the late 1800s, a British mining syndicate mined for silver in (where else?) Silver Canyon and mining got another big boost during the Wrigley era in the 1920s.

The Blackjack Mine, for example, reached its heyday during the Roaring '20s. Lead, silver and zinc were extracted from the mine and carried by ore cart along a precipitous skyway down to the processing facility at White's Landing where the finished material was then taken by barge to the mainland. (I remember many years ago talking to a former Blackjack miner who told me that their transportation to and from the worksite each day was a thrilling ride aboard these carts. That alone would make the hours of underground toil and labor worthwhile!)

Catalina's mining era ended in 1927 with the closure of all mines on the Island, due mostly to the collapse of prices on world metals markets. But as noted earlier, the above-ground workings still exist and much of the labyrinth of tunnels they left behind still lie hidden beneath the topsoil.

A widely-known mine on the Island's East End that was shut down in the 1920s still has a number of rusting mining carts strewn about. Its ancient wooden towers with their wire rope running off into the undergrowth are still there, entangled in vines and rotting away in the jungle like some abandoned colonial operation in the Belgian Congo.

I remember talking to a former resident of the Island who told me of a camping trip she took one time into another one of Catalina's mines. This particular mine was one of those partially submerged mines where a portion of her subterranean adventure took her through an underground pool. Knowing this ahead of time, she packed her goods in a dry bag and set off.

After entering the mine and successfully fording the underground reservoir, she set up camp in a little recess. I remember her telling me she sat up all night inside her little dome tent absolutely terrified because "something" was in the mine with her—something "big." She refused to go to sleep or step out of her tent for fear of encountering whatever creature was sharing the cavern with her that night.

The whereabouts of most of the Island's mines are well known, thanks to good old-fashioned record-keeping. However, some of these caverns apparently escaped this diligence as evidenced by a fascinating discovery I made several years ago—a discovery not made on Catalina Island, but in a used book store in Long Beach…

THE MOST MYSTERIOUS MINE OF ALL

Many years ago, for reasons long forgotten, I found myself spending a rainy night in Long Beach after missing the last boat to the Island. Since there was a convention in town, the lack of any sort of affordable accommodations in the downtown area drove me to one of those seedy bungalow motels that color the harbor's hectic stretches of the renowned Pacific Coast Highway.

In an effort to escape my vintage surroundings and to temporarily cure the "overtown lonelies" I paid a visit that evening to that most wonderful (but unfortunately now defunct) used bookstore, the one that proudly advertised "acres of books."

For perhaps an hour and a half I perused many a quaint and curious volume of forgotten lore, from History to Foreign Languages and Travel and, finally, to Geology.

Here, amongst dusty bound volumes that told of plate tectonics, mineral exploration and volcanic mayhem, was a book that looked quite out of place. The topic of the book itself wasn't "out of place." It was simply labeled *Mines*. What made it out of place was that it looked to be nothing more than a worn journal of sorts, not a commercially bound book. Imagine my surprise when I opened it up and found it was about mines on Catalina Island!

Now, this was a book that I had to have for my collection. So I paid my three dollars and tax or whatever and, with bagged book under arm, disappeared into the rainy neon streets of Long Beach.

Upon first reading the journal, whose entries dated almost exclusively to the 1920s, I found most of its contents to be nothing more than dry tabulations of mining statistics, ore values, calculations of daily drilling distances, etcetera, for the various mines around the Island, including Blackjack, Johnson's Landing, 4th of July Cove and several others.

But then one particular entry caught my eye. Unlike the entries for the other mines, this entry for the "Santa Catalina Copper Prospect" was written text or prose, not tables and tabulations. Whoever wrote this entry evidently had something different to say about *this* mine.

The entry detailed the efforts of two miners who were following what they hoped would be a worthwhile vein of copper. "Accordingly," reads the journal, "two miners started drifting this cut along a dyke, or vein, April 18, 1925."

After prospecting this vein for a while, the miners came to the conclusion that the real meat of this lode must be down deeper. So they gathered their gear and headed downhill "50 feet vertically below" where they began opening a new tunnel. It is here, that they made a remarkable and mysterious discovery.

"Advancing 16 feet on second tunnel," reads the journal, "the miners broke thru' into 'something'."

This "something," according to the journal, was described as an "apparently 'prehistoric' tunnel. Driven great many years ago."

Upon further exploration into this mysterious tunnel, the miners found that it went back more than 100 feet into the mountain where they found a "very ancient" solid iron shovel.

What exactly did these miners find? While there were many mines driven into the hills of Silver Canyon and the West End back in the 1800s, there is no record whatsoever of any hard rock mining in this particular location until the 1920s.

Adding to the mystery is the fact that the miners in the journal were no doubt professionals who had likely descended from a long line of miners possibly dating back to the Old Country, and yet even they had no idea what they had found. The simple fact that they describe the tunnel as "prehistoric" and "driven great many years ago" is revealing and even startling.

Why was the ancient mine dug in the first place? It evidently wasn't to mine copper, since the 1920s miners still had to prospect the copper ore within this mine. In other words, the "mystery miners" who drove the original tunnel were apparently uninterested in the copper ore and simply passed it by. What were they looking for?

My next step was to try to determine the location of the mine based on the coordinates given in the journal—coordinates that basically amounted to elevation and distance from a well-known location on the Island, whose name I won't divulge. (It is NOT the Casino).

I then sat at my computer and loaded Google Earth. On the satellite image of Catalina, I anchored the ruler tool on this undivulge-able Catalina location and swept it back and forth until I hit the 300-foot elevation mark a distance of 1,500 feet away as prescribed in the journal.

There, before my eyes in a modern-day Google Earth image, were the tailings and cast-off rocks and dirt from the mine scattered down the hillside.

I have yet to visit the "Santa Catalina Copper Prospect" and despite the fact that the tailings are still there, in all likelihood the entrance was sealed up long ago as evidenced by the final entry in the journal. After several days of prospecting, it seems the miners decided the payoff wouldn't be worth beginning full scale mining operations and the project was given up.

"As the magnitude of this source is very questionable," reads the journal, "it was decided to abandon the prospect for all time."

So the question remains, what was the purpose of this mine and who is responsible for digging it in the first place?

For a really out-of-this-world theory on the possible origins of our "mystery mine" I suggest you read (or re-read) the segment "Land of the Giants" in Chapter 3.

THE HUNT FOR TURIE'S TREASURE

On a Spring day in 1829, a New England-native named Samuel Prentiss, carpenter by trade, found himself sitting alone on a wind-swept beach on Catalina's West End.

He was, quite possibly, the only soul on Catalina Island at that particular moment. The Island Tongva had by this time vanished from their ancestral homeland, "recruited" for jobs in mainland missions and ranchos, and most of the white miners and goat herders were still a few years away from establishing their enterprises on Catalina.

In the preceding six months, Prentiss had left his home, lost his girlfriend, lost all the tools of his trade and very nearly lost his life in two separate shipwrecks, the last of which found him stranded on Catalina.

What was this poor castaway possibly going to do now? Why, dig for buried treasure, of course!

The story of Samuel Prentiss and his hunt for a fabled treasure purportedly belonging to an Island chieftain named Turie (or possibly Turia), has all the elements of a great "lost treasure" story. Perhaps *too many* great elements, in fact, and the truth may have been quite different from the story that has been handed down through the past two centuries.

Nevertheless, it is one of my favorites in a lifetime of pursuing such tales and if only half of it is true it rightfully deserves its place in Island lore.

Our story begins on Christmas Eve 1828 aboard the Yankee brig *Danube* anchored off the coast of Point Fermin in San Pedro.

It was, as they say, a dark and stormy night, and a vicious southeaster had sprung up leaving the *Danube* no time to get under way. She was very quickly run aground at a place ominously called Dead Man's Island and, according to the legend, all hands were lost, save four sailors, including our hero Mr. Prentiss.

Prentiss, who had left his home and his sweetheart back east, had joined the *Danube* in Peru after deserting an American man-of-war in South America. No doubt, he was feeling the Hand of Providence at this point.

The survivors of the wreck made their way to what passed for civilization on the California coast in those days and Prentiss eventually found himself at Mission San Gabriel. Here, it is said, he befriended the dying Chief Turie who divulged to him the location of an enormously valuable treasure buried on Catalina Island reportedly interred in Turie's old stomping grounds by the English privateer Sir Thomas Cavendish.

Prentiss eventually made his way back to the wreck of the *Danube*, still strewn about the beaches of San Pedro. Turning his carpentry skills to hand, he fashioned himself a small sloop in between occasional glances at the distant silhouette of Catalina which he believed held his yet-to-be-discovered treasure.

In the Spring of 1829, Prentiss' craft was ready for sea and preparations were made for the voyage across the channel. But the sea had a few more tricks in store for the young carpenter.

Halfway across the channel, it is said, a fickle wind blew his crude treasure map overboard and into the sea. Not satisfied with this, the devious Northwesterly winds proceeded to kick up the seas enough to swamp Prentiss' little boat, sending it to the bottom along with all of Prentiss' provisions and carpentry tools.

Prentiss, who was apparently better at swimming than sailing, eventually dragged his weary bones upon the shores of Catalina's West End. Foodless, shelterless and—perhaps most painful to Prentiss—mapless, he no doubt scanned the lonely scrub-oak hills of Catalina and wondered what was to become of him. The only thing he remembered from the map was that the treasure was buried "under a tree."

Undeterred by this latest catastrophe, Prentiss rolled up his sea-soaked sleeves and began his new life: a treasure-hunting life that would span another thirty years.

Having lost his treasure map, Prentiss set about searching for this legendary treasure while supporting himself chiefly through hunting and fishing, at least during the early years when he had little company and consequently few people with whom to trade.

While searching for the buried treasure, Prentiss came across small yields of silver ore and even a few gold flakes now and then. In between searching for the legendary treasure, reportedly buried by pirates centuries before, he calculated he could at least earn some money on the side.

Not much is known about these years in Prentiss' life, but one can imagine seeing him swinging his pickaxe and scooping his shovel beneath the boughs of countless oaks and toyons.

The days rolled into months and the months rolled into years and decades and despite all his efforts, Prentiss never did find his treasure. He passed away in 1854, and is buried just outside of Two Harbors—purportedly the first white man to be buried on the Island.

According to the legend, however, his secret did not die with him. Like Chief Turie three decades before, it is said that a dying Prentiss passed his secret on to a new character who entered the scene by the name of Santos Louis Bouchette.

Anyone familiar with the Two Harbors and West End area of the Island will recognize the name Bouchette as the name of one of the mines in the area as well as name of the road that winds along the lee shore of that part of the Island.

Now, Santos Bouchette was a little more of a businessman than our friend Prentiss, who was content to be something of a drifter and loner; an "unlettered bachelor" as he was referred to years later.

Bouchette began a small-scale mining operation under the Bouchette Small Hills mining claim while secretly searching for Turie's lost treasure in his spare time.

Businessman Bouchette, in fact, went so far as to enlist the help of mainland financiers to aid him in his endeavors. With his ore assaying in at between $200 and $800 per ton, it was not difficult to get backers.

(One part of the legend says that a crafty Bouchette often "salted" his mines with gold dust and nuggets before treating potential investors to a tour. He would then conveniently "find" the gold while regaling the VIP with tales of the fortunes to be made.)

In just this manner, Bouchette went on for many years until his story takes a decidedly juicier turn with the introduction of a "lovely French dancer" he met on one of his junkets to Los Angeles.

Bouchette was smitten and, after marrying the young woman, brought her to the Island. Unfortunately for Bouchette, however, his new femme disliked Island life and longed to return to the bright gas lamps of Los Angeles.

In an effort to keep his new wife happy, Bouchette built a house at the Isthmus and endeavored to furnish it as lavishly as possible with furniture and a plate-glass mirror imported from France. The strategy evidently worked and the two settled down to married life at Johnson's Landing.

In the background, mind you, Mr. Bouchette was continuously searching for the buried treasure, all the while presumably keeping it a secret from his workers, if not his wife.

Then the day came, as the legend says, that Santos Louis Bouchette and his wife, suddenly and without prior notification to anyone, packed up their belongings, loaded up a longboat and sailed away toward the mainland—never to be seen again.

Had Bouchette found Turie's treasure? If so, had he only recently discovered it? Or perhaps he had found it long before and had just been biding his time, stowing bits and pieces of it away quietly so as not to alert his workers.

Or perhaps Bouchette came up as empty as Prentiss had. Perhaps he had simply tired of the life of a miner and—tired as well of being harangued by his wife—finally threw in the towel.

Or...

Or perhaps there never was buried treasure to begin with. Perhaps there never was a treasure map scrawled by a dying Indian chieftain who perhaps never even existed.

Perhaps the entire story had been concocted by Prentiss (with or without Bouchette's knowledge and subsequent collaboration) as a means of luring potential investors into his fledgling mining business, a strategy that appears to have been successful, if that's what he was up to.

Of course, at this late date we'll probably never really know the truth—unless, of course, someone finds the treasure some day.

Otherwise, the answer to whether or not the legend is real or simply made up was taken to the grave by a New England-native named Samuel Prentiss, carpenter by trade, who lies in a simple grave beneath a simple headstone overlooking the sea.

Mysterious Deaths
(and close calls!)

From Natalie Wood to a Nazi war criminal, Catalina has seen its share of mysterious deaths and disappearances. Although all of the following cases have been thoroughly investigated by everyone from law enforcement officials to the media to private individuals, most of them will likely never be solved,

NATALIE WOOD

While Catalina Island generally receives favorable press worldwide and is looked upon as a happy place, free of the world's cares, from time to time an event occurs on the Island that generates tragic headlines.

Such an event was the untimely death in 1981 of Hollywood movie legend Natalie Wood at Two Harbors on Catalina's West End.

According to official accounts of the event, at 3 a.m. on November 29, 1981, Wood was said to have disappeared after going on the deck of the yacht belonging to her and her husband, Robert Wagner. Actor Christopher Walken was also on board.

Several witnesses on other boats in the area reported they heard arguing board Wagner's vessel earlier that night. Wagner himself told police the two had had an argument but had "calmed down" before going to bed.

At some point during the night, Wood went up on deck and after some time had passed without her return. Noticing their small inflatable dinghy gone, Wagner went looking for her in another boat. Unable to find her anywhere in the dark, he notified the local Harbor Patrol who also looked in vain for her.

As the fruitless search wore on through the night, Doug Bombard, general manager for all business operations in the Two Harbors area at the time, was enlisted to join in the search.

"They'd been looking all night and they came up and got me about just a half hour before dawn," he said. "What they told me they thought happened is that she slipped and fell into the water during the night about 3 a.m."

By the time Doug was awakened, searchers had recovered the inflatable dinghy. But Natalie was nowhere to be found.

Knowing the ocean currents in the area as well or better than anyone, Doug first checked the kelp line along the east shore of Isthmus Harbor.

As he rounded Blue Cavern Point, Doug noticed a small red-colored "bubble" floating on the surface about 100 yards offshore. The red bubble turned out to be a pocket of air in Natalie's red down jacket. There, he found Natalie's body hanging feet first under the water by the jacket's straps.

"I hung onto her," said Doug, "and she was heavy. Her lungs were full of water and she was hanging underneath the jacket."

Doug described her as being dressed in mukluk-style boots with a long night gown.

"I hung onto her and called one of my shoreboats," he said. "One of (the shoreboats) came in and helped me lift her into the boat."

By the time Doug found her she "was long gone," he said, adding that "With that water as cold as it is there was no rigor mortis."

Afterwards, Doug went out to Wagner's boat to tell him the news. "I went and told him what I found and he didn't say much."

About 45 minutes later, Wagner and Walken came into Doug's office at the foot of the pier at Isthmus Harbor and told him "what they thought happened."

Wagner told Doug they had been out to dinner at the Bombard's restaurant, Doug's Harbor Reef. Afterwards, they returned to their yacht in the inflatable and then tied the dinghy to the yacht's stern cleat. Then, both Wagner and Wood went below and eventually went to bed.

Wagner then told Doug that he believed Natalie got up in the middle of the night to retie the dinghy to the cleat. "He was guessing that what she probably did, was that the dinghy would be banging against the side of the boat and they had an aft stateroom." It was while Natalie was retying the dinghy line that she fell in, said Wagner.

Doug doesn't give much credence to recent stories that Wagner was somehow at fault, possibly even guilty of murder.

"Basically what he (Wagner) told me makes sense," he said.

Equally implausible to Doug is that Natalie, out of anger, got into the inflatable on her own to motor around in the night.

"I'll guarantee you she wasn't out for a night running around in the inflatable. That wasn't her bag at all. She wasn't real nuts about being out on the water," he added. "She wasn't a swimmer. She was always up on the bow sunning herself."

The case of Natalie Wood's drowning was re-opened on the 30th anniversary of her death in 2011, although authorities at the time came to the conclusion that there was no new evidence to contradict the original conclusion.

However, in a surprise announcement in July 2012 the Los Angeles County Coroner's office changed the cause of death from "accident drowning" to "undetermined." The reason for the change was stated as being "some of the bruises on Wood's body were inconsistent with death by drowning."

MURDER AT THE METROPOLE

The people of Catalina enjoy one of the most crime-free environments in the world. Violent crime in particular is exceedingly rare and one could nearly count the number of homicides that have occurred in the past century on one hand. Well, maybe two hands.

But people are still people wherever you go and from time to time someone feels the need to deprive a fellow human of his or her life.

Such was the case with an incident that occurred many years ago in the old Hotel Metropole, Catalina Island's oldest hotel. And while the murder itself has never been a secret, even in such an image-oriented destination as Catalina, a mysterious new twist emerged recently; a twist that comes compliments of our local friend and barber *extraordinaire* Lolo Saldana.

It was in the early morning hours of August 12, 1902, that a shot rang out in one of the hotel's private parlors, behind whose doors a poker game was being played.

A man named Harry Johnson raced from the room to report that another gambler, Alfred Boyd, had shot and killed professional gambler W.A. Yaeger, a.k.a. "The St. Louis Sport."

To make a long story short, Boyd was charged with the murder, but was eventually found not guilty thanks to a variety of then-untested courtroom theatrics that were so revolutionary that the defense attorney, Earl Rogers, would later become the inspiration for Erle Stanley Gardner's "Perry Mason" character of novels, film and television.

Both Johnson and Boyd testified during the trial and although Boyd was found innocent, it has long been assumed that it was one of the two who had committed the murder.

But could there have been a third suspect involved?

Enter Lolo and his new twist on the story:

"Back in the early 1960s, I was cutting an elderly man's hair one day and he said 'You guys have ruined this town'," said Lolo.

Somewhat taken aback by this comment, Lolo asked what the gentlemen meant by his remark.

"You've ruined it with that big round building," said the man, evidently referring to the Casino. Upon further questioning, Lolo learned that the gentleman had lived on the Island many years before; not only before the present-day Casino, but even before its predecessor, the old Sugarloaf Casino.

He went on to tell Lolo that he had considered Descanso Bay a prime fishing spot back in the day and that somehow the construction of the Casino had ruined it.

Although he was having trouble making the connection between the presence of the Casino and the ruination of a fishing hole (fish don't like Art Deco?), Lolo was nevertheless interested in the man's early connections with Avalon. So he carried the conversation further, snipping the man's hair as he did so.

The mysterious customer told Lolo that his family actually lived in the Metropole at the turn of the century and that his father was a regular "customer" at the poker tables in the hotel's private rooms. Early one summer morning (the man didn't remember the date), he was hastily awakened by his mother.

"Get up!," she said. "Pack your bags, we're leaving the Island!"

Lolo said the man then related how his mother told him they were leaving "for good" and heading to Canada and he was admonished to "never return to Catalina again." The family then proceeded to vacate their Island home in the pale light of an impending dawn.

For more than 60 years—during which time the man never learned the reason for his family's exodus—the man heeded his mother's advice, all the while maintaining residency in Canada. It wasn't until the 1960s, impelled by that desire that overcomes so many in their twilight years to revisit the stomping grounds of their youth, that he made one last pilgrimage to Catalina and landed in Lolo's chair.

Could this man's father have committed the murder or somehow been involved in it? It's certainly possible his father's motive for abandoning the Island was unrelated to the killing, although such a hasty and involved retreat smacks of something more sinister than a simple gambling debt or a fling with another man's lady.

After nearly half a century, Lolo doesn't recall the man's name, if in fact it was ever even divulged to him. But his tale either sheds light on—or perhaps deepens—the mystery of the Murder at the Metropole.

A MOST DISTURBING DISCOVERY

Several years ago while doing research for my various "mysterious" projects on Catalina history, I paid a visit to a relatively new hotel on the Island. Like most of Catalina's hotels, this one occupied a building which had been standing in Avalon for nearly a century.

I was given a brief tour of the property by an enthusiastic employee whom I shall refer to as "Carlos."

Carlos gave me the grand tour of the newly-renovated property, a tour which ended up in the hotel's finest suite, a dazzling Japanese-style affair with a fireplace, huge wall-mounted flatscreen and so forth.

As is my usual custom, I eventually got to the heart of my visit. "You got any ghost stories about this hotel?"

There was a pause.

"Well," he answered. "Not really a ghost story, but…"

Carlos then went on to regale me with a tale of one of his first days on the job when he was helping with the drastic make-over the place was getting. The plan for the new hotel was to clear out the crawl space beneath the building to make room for office space which would be used by the hotel. I think you know where this is going.

One day, Carlos was excavating the ground beneath the very room in which we were both standing, when he first came upon a pair of women's panties. Interesting, he thought. He kept digging.

Shortly afterwards, he uncovered a woman's bra. He kept digging.

Not long after that, to his horror, he uncovered "lots and lots of dried blood."

"You sure it wasn't just old dried red paint or something?," I asked.

"No," he insisted. "It was blood."

No human remains were ever found in the excavation or, if they were found they were never reported.

If there was a indeed a murder involved it was never reported as no such event is connected with this particular address. Assuming there was a secret killing, you may ask yourself how someone could simply disappear in a small town such as Avalon anyone raising a ruckus.

Part of the answer could be that it is believed that about a century ago the building was a "gentleman's club." Despite often respectable fronts to such enterprises, prostitution was not uncommon and the death or disappearance of a call girl from L.A. would not be noticed locally.

Therefore, it's entirely conceivable that, once upon a time, someone at this "gentleman's club" was not a gentleman.

THE SHOCKING SECRET
OF THE 1915 FIRE

It seems that all great cities of the world have at one time or another suffered a great, disastrous fire in their distant histories. Long before the advent of modern fire safety practices and firefighting technology, most of the world's populated centers have a history of suffering such a conflagration.

There was the Great Fire of London in 1666, which destroyed more than 90 percent of London's central district known as The City. There was the Great Fire of New York in 1776, only two months after the Declaration of Independence; a fire which destroyed as much as one-quarter of the city of New York.

Most well-known of all, perhaps, is the Great Chicago Fire of 1871, which killed hundreds and leveled nearly 3½ square miles of the Windy City.

Avalon (being one of the world's great cities) is no different. It was on November 29, 1915, that we made our contribution to the world's "great fires" list when a blaze got started in the Rose Hotel located about where the Hotel Villa Portofino is now and proceeded to destroy nearly 1/3 of the town, including the palatial Hotel Metropole.

The media of the day and the common sentiment over the decades since has concluded that the fire began as a simple kitchen fire in a café located in, or near, the Rose Hotel.

But a voice from the past, barely audible on an old oral history cassette tape from the 1970s, has perhaps revealed a terrible secret behind the 1915 fire; the kind of secret of which nightmares are made. That voice belonged to none other than Johnny Windle, one of Avalon's most respected founding citizens.

The son of Judge Ernest Windle, who in between hearing cases at the bench found time to establish and operate the *Catalina Islander* newspaper, Johnny Windle was as close to a town patriarch as a town can have. He was a plain-speaking, hard-working individual who held various positions of importance in Catalina history and directly participated in many of Avalon's most momentous events. To those who knew him, his reputation on Catalina Island was sterling.

During the 1970s, Catalina Islander Chuck Liddell tirelessly documented early Avalon history with dozens of oral history interviews with early residents, from Jessie McClanahan to Squirrel D'Arcy to Jimmy Trout and many others. These tapes are now the property of the Catalina Island Museum.

One of Chuck's interviews, conducted in 1978, was with Johnny Windle and included a lengthy segment on Mr. Windle's experiences in the 1915 fire.

At 2:30 a.m. on November 29, young Johnny was abruptly awakened by the town constable, Al Wiggs. "Fire! Fire!," yelled Wiggs. Johnny ran into the street in the early morning darkness and beheld his town in flames. "It looked like the whole town was going," said Windle in the interview. "That's exactly how it looked to everybody.

"You look to where the (Cabrillo) Mole is now," he continued, "and it was nothing but women and children trying to get away from the fire."

Citizens gathered their belongings in push carts and bed sheets and filed zombie-like towards the safety of the east side of town. The windows in the stately Hotel Metropole exploded in the heat and the Moricich family pushed their piano out of the house and straight up Stage Coach Road. "People were doing things they would never be able to do if everything was all right," said Windle.

But it is after Windle finishes his general narrative of the fire that things in the interview really get interesting.

"OK," said interviewer Chuck Liddell on the tape. "Is that the end of the fire story then?"

There is a pause.

"Well, no," answered Windle, "There's one more item…"

Windle then goes on to describe how he was told by Tinch Moricich and Squirrel D'Arcy about how, in the midst of the maelstrom, they had to rescue the mother-in-law of the owner of the Rose Hotel, who had evidently been INTENTIONALLY locked in the attic. Moricich, who would later become town constable, had to bust open a padlock and force a trap door open to free the woman, injuring his shoulder in the process.

Windle then goes on to say how the woman's son-in-law had, only days before the fire, curiously begun to move his belongings out of the hotel.

"Let me get this straight then," asked Chuck bluntly in the interview. "We're assuming (the son-in-law) locked the mother-in-law in there to do away with her."

"You can assume what you want," replied Johnny.

Heavy stuff. Stuff that gets a lot heavier when you also consider that only four hours before the fire began, another mysterious fire had been set on the other end of town at 200 Eucalyptus Street. This previous fire had drawn all of Avalon's volunteer fire department and their equipment to the other side of town.

This equipment was evidently not put back in order before the main fire broke out at the Rose. In fact, the *Los Angeles Times* story even mentions that efforts to fight the Rose Hotel fire were greatly hampered by the fact that "most of the hose and firefighting gear was still up at Eucalyptus."

Was Avalon's Great Fire of 1915 intentionally set by the owner of the Rose Hotel? If so, was it done for insurance purposes or—chillingly—to "do away" with an inconvenient mother-in-law?

Was the Eucalyptus Street fire set intentionally as a diversion, knowing that the volunteer firefighters would be ill-prepared and perhaps too beat to fight a second, bigger fire in town? (The L.A. District Attorney reportedly came out to investigate the story, but without result).

As is often the case with these little unpolished gems of history that are unearthed, all living memory and any semblance of documentation is now and forever gone, so we'll probably never know the truth.

In the words of the legendary Johnny Windle, "you can assume what you want."

THOMAS HARPER INCE

Catalina Island, being so close to the burgeoning Hollywood film industry, naturally has figured prominently into the Babylonistic lifestyles of the movie producers, stars and starlets of that industry.

The Island's proximity to Los Angeles and its tropical (or at least sub-tropical) mystique made the Island a perfect playground for the movers and shakers of Hollywood.

Director Thomas Harper Ince was an established player in the motion picture industry in those days and the reason you've probably never heard of him is largely due to a tragic series of events on or about the evening of November 15, 1924; a mysterious set of circumstances that whisked him away from the hot lights of the Hollywood stage and into the cold, hard ground.

Had it not been for the events on that fateful eve, his name may well have been as prominent as Cecil B. DeMille or D.W. Griffith, as Ince had already begun to secure a name for himself as a revolutionary and far-sighted director.

The death of Ince and its connection to Catalina is admittedly tenuous, but it is believed that Catalina was the ultimate destination of the yacht on this particular voyage.

But Ince's connections with the Island are clear. In fact, his film *Civilization*, considered by many to be his crowning achievement, was partially filmed on the Island, most notably the inclusion in the film of a smoldering Avalon following the devastating 1915 fire.

So onboard the *Oneida*, the stage for Ince's death was set. The actors in this scene included not only William Randolph Hearst, but silent film stars Charlie Chaplin and Marion Davies along with the usual entourage of columnists, lesser-known stars and general Hollywood groupies.

The *Oneida* had sailed from San Pedro to San Diego and it was there that Ince joined the party, having arrived by train earlier in the day.

It is said that at some point during the evening, Ince was taken ashore with a "stomach ailment." From this point on, the tale diverges from a simple gastrointestinal problem to a tabloid murder.

One way or the other, by most accounts, Ince was dead within 24 hours.

The Hollywood press immediately seized on (or perhaps created) a story of Ince's death by pistol at the hands of an enraged Hearst, who—it was reported—lusted after Marion Davies. "Movie Producer Shot on Hearst Yacht!," screamed the *Los Angeles Times*.

The wild media speculation (fueled, it is said, by Hearst's numerous enemies) essentially morphed into a number of different stories: that Hearst found Ince and Davies in an uncompromising position in the ship's galley and pulled out his gat and started shooting; that Hearst found Chaplin and Davies in an uncompromising position, pulled out his pistol and accidentally shot through the bulkhead, hitting an innocent Ince in the adjoining cabin; or that Ince, hearing the shots in the first scenario, came to the rescue of Chaplin, only to be shot himself.

As exciting as all this sounds, the truth appears to be quite different. Nevertheless, conspiracy theories abounded along with some interesting tidbits of hearsay that would bolster those theories.

The first account was purportedly from Chaplin's secretary, Toraichi Kono, who supposedly helped Ince off the yacht. Kono claimed that the stricken man was decidedly afflicted with a gunshot wound to the head.

Then there were the various differing accounts from many of the celebrities themselves on the yacht that night, including Chaplin and Davies, who claimed that they visited a decidedly *living* Ince two weeks after the alleged incident and that Ince was never actually on board the yacht in the first place.

Additionally, no formal inquest or autopsy was supposedly ever performed (the body was cremated within 24 hours) and the District Attorney in charge of the case never interviewed any of the people on the yacht.

Add to that the interesting rumor that Hearst silently paid up the mortgage on Ince's Hollywood townhouse some time later.

"All you have to do to make Hearst turn white as a ghost," said famed movie producer D.W. Griffith later, "is to mention Ince's name.

"There's plenty wrong there," said Griffith. "But Hearst is too big."

As with most conspiracy theories, it is the romantic tales of such events that survive the years and not the truth. *The Cat's Meow*, a major motion picture directed by none other than Peter Bogdanovich further carried the conspiracy theory to its ridiculous ends.

But Brian Taves, author of *Thomas Ince: Hollywood's Independent Pioneer* convincibly asserts that Ince was very much alive until his return home from the fateful yacht trip until there, in his own home, he died of a heart attack.

Nevertheless, the conspiracy theories survive, unfortunately tainting the legend of one of Hollywood's most brilliant young directors.

JIM WATSON

THE STRANGE DISAPPEARANCE
OF GUSTAVE CARLSTROM

The only reason I didn't name this segment "The Strange DEATH of Gustave Carlstrom" is, quite simply, because the body of this 45-year-old Swedish immigrant, shoemaker and early Avalon curio vendor, supposedly somewhere out in the hills, has to this day never been found.

But back in the wild and wooly days of Avalon's early history, such discrepancies—and the wherewithal to resolve them—were not uncommon. The Island's interior was still considered something of a wilderness back then and, after all, accidents do happen; assuming, of course, that the reported demise of Carlstrom was indeed an accident...

In 1888, Avalon was still a town in its infancy. Spreading across the salty grasses and marshes of Avalon Canyon was a collection of several dozen tents made of stiff canvas that flapped lazily in the afternoon winds like the ship's sails many of them had once been.

Above it all stood the palatial Hotel Metropole, brand-spanking new and still smelling of fresh cut lumber and new paint. Within this bastion of civilization at the corner of Metropole and Crescent, uniformed cooks, waiters, maids and assorted service personnel busied themselves daily with the task of feeding and housing the many visitors that arrived on the soot-belching steamers from San Pedro.

Just up the hill from the "Met" on Whittley Avenue, about where the Avalon Hotel now stands, Carlstrom eked out his living by doing odd jobs for neighbors and by polishing a variety of seashells he culled from the nearby beaches; shells that he would later sell to visitors.

Although the steamers *S.S. Falcon* and the short-lived *S.S. Ferndale* brought most of the food for the town and its visitors, local residents supplemented vegetable inventories with gardens, and hunting parties helped furnish additional meat.

It was in early December 1888 that just such a hunting party was formed; a party that included both Carlstrom and another Swedish immigrant named Sven Anderson, along with several other townsmen.

84

In the parlance of the day, Anderson was "less alert" than most and this mentally-challenged state of his was the cause of no end of pranks and practical jokes from the other young men in town.

Though older and of sounder mind than Anderson, Carlstrom himself had very little experience in the ways of guns and hunting and it took a great deal of pleading and cajoling on the part of the two Swedes to be allowed to tag along. But consent was finally and reluctantly given and the party headed out on horseback north to the Summit above Avalon and then along the creek down into Middle Canyon where they spent the night.

While the hunting party was loathe to allow either Anderson or Carlstrom a chance to use their hunting rifles, they once again succumbed to the pleading of the two and decided to let Anderson have a crack at shooting several wild cattle that happened along at one point in their journey. To their great amusement, the rest of the party watched as Anderson emptied the entire contents of his lever-action Winchester without hitting a damn thing.

Now, a man who can't hit anything he's aiming at is, by inference, a man who is hitting things that he's NOT aiming at and it was decided for safety reasons to allow Anderson and Carlstrom to continue their end of the hunt on their own, separate from the group. The other hunters went off in a safer direction, while Anderson and Carlstrom wandered away on their own and straight into the annals of Catalina's unsolved mysteries.

It was late that evening, as the hunting party sat around a crackling campfire somewhere in Middle Canyon, that Anderson showed up. He was alone.

Anderson explained that he did not know where Carlstrom was or what had happened to him. Despite the late hour, Hunt demanded that Anderson retrace his steps and continue looking for his fellow countryman until he found him.

Joe Adargo, one of the other hunters, convinced Hunt that the rest of the party should set out on horseback and look on their own for the missing man, which they did to no avail. After returning to camp, they anxiously waited for either Anderson or Carlstrom, or both, to return.

Finally, the flickering campfire light once again illuminated the nervous face of Anderson, who had returned to announce that he had found Carlstrom's body. He had been so late in returning, he explained, because he had taken time to bury the man.

This was too much for the party and once again they mounted their horses and headed off, this time to look for the burial site. But Anderson either couldn't or *wouldn't* remember the location and the disheartened party returned to Avalon to report the sad news.

Back in town the next day, the startled townsfolk put together a hasty "trial" for Anderson, complete with the Hotel Metropole manager, a man named Adams, acting as judge. There was no official law yet in Avalon—much less a jail—and evidently the Island's owner, George Shatto, was not present or he surely would have presided over the matter.

After much examination and cross-examination, the "jury" eventually decided that Carlstrom had perished of "hunger and thirst," a startling conclusion given that the man had only been out in the hills for a day or two. Anderson's only crime, it was decided, was in "burying a body without a witness."

Anderson was released and allowed back to his tent, although whatever psychological torment to which he had been subject by the young men in town to date was now greatly amplified.

Did Anderson accidentally shoot Carlstrom and bury the body to cover his transgression? Did he outright murder the man?

Or perhaps Anderson and Carlstrom did get separated from one another, as Anderson originally stated. And maybe Anderson really did find the dead Carlstrom (fall? heart attack?) only on his second trip out into the woods, although it's rather odd that he decided at that moment to bury the man in the dark of night rather than make his way back to the hunting party to report his findings. Was he hiding something? A bullet wound perhaps?

There is much we don't know about the town and its occupants in those days. Anderson's "acquittal" may have been the result of sympathy for him and his mental condition. Perhaps no one seriously believed he was capable of murder. Going hand in hand with that, perhaps Carlstrom was a man who was disliked by the community, thereby dampening anyone's enthusiasm for the truth.

We'll probably never know the answers to these questions, as they are buried somewhere out in the hills, perhaps beneath the boughs of an old willow tree, in a shallow grave carved out by bare hands and the butt end of a Winchester repeater.

WARTIME & MILITARY MYSTERIES

Like the rest of America, Catalina Island answered the call to duty during the Second World War. Below are just a small number of the many mysteries and amazing stories that occurred during that global conflict along with a more recent mystery.

THE MYSTERIOUS GOLFERS

It's common knowledge around town that our local barber Lolo Saldana has spent many years of his life working in and promoting sports and recreation on the Island, from coaching baseball teams to writing sports columns in this very newspaper.

But what few people know about Lolo is his possible brush with the world of covert military surveillance while performing one of his earliest endeavors in the local sporting world as a caddy at the Catalina Island Golf Course.

It was on a summer's day in July of 1941, six months before the attack on Pearl Harbor, when Lolo and his friend Conrad were given the task of caddying for an unusual pair of golfers.

"It just so happened these two Japanese men came up and they had cameras and stuff like that and we got the job of caddying for them," said Lolo.

The first thing that Lolo noticed was the unusual way the gentlemen were dressed. Even though it was a warm July day, they were wearing black suits and ties—at the golf course.

After play got under way, another thing became obvious to Lolo: these men had no interest in playing golf and, in fact, seemed to have no knowledge of the game whatsoever. Instead, they seemed to be interested only in the local terrain and were decidedly only going through the *motions* of playing golf.

"My friend Conrad and I took them out," said Lolo, "and these guys kept taking pictures of the hillsides and talking and pointing and doing things like that. Well, they were talking in Japanese and we didn't know what they were saying."

The bizarre round of golf—complete with note-taking and photographing—continued until the gentlemen seemed satisfied and went on their merry way.

Six months later, in a series of blitzkriegs around the Pacific, the Empire of Japan attacked not only Pearl Harbor, but Hong Kong, Singapore, the Philippines, Wake Island and a number of other locations.

While the dreaded invasion of the West Coast never materialized, the Imperial Japanese Navy dispatched three submarines to patrol the waters around Catalina and the coast of Southern California. Japanese submarines I-17, I-19 and I-21 all wreaked their own brand of havoc on U.S. shipping along the coast, striking as close to Catalina as the mouth of Los Angeles Harbor and the Elwood oil storage facility north of Santa Barbara.

Sightings of Japanese submarines in the channel were not uncommon.

Were Lolo's golfers a vanguard of sorts for these assaults? Although it wasn't until after the war that Lolo recalled the strange events at the golf course, there is no doubt in his mind what these fellows were up to.

"These guys were sent here to spy," he said. "They knew what they were going to do on Catalina."

Since this incident was never reported, it is unlikely that the U.S. government ever knew about it. Perhaps somewhere in a dusty filing cabinet in a basement somewhere in Tokyo, one might find the scribbled notes and photographs taken by the "golfers." But the Island doesn't give up her secrets easily and the true mission of the Japanese golfers may never be discovered.

THE IMPERIAL JAPANESE CHRISTMAS

Christmas time is a magical time on Catalina. Once again the yuletide holidays overtake the Island and once again carols are tolled in the old Chimes Tower on the hill overlooking the Casino. Decorations and dazzling light displays line Front Street in a holiday tradition that has existed in Avalon in one form or another since Christmas of 1887.

But the Christmas of 1941 was very different from any other for Catalina as well as the rest of the nation.

Within two weeks of the December 7, 1941, attack on Pearl Harbor, all tourist travel to the Island was terminated for the four-year duration of the war and cross-channel travel was severely restricted even for resident Islanders.

While the Allied powers were at war with a number of Axis powers, for Catalina and the West Coast the primary entity that generated sleepless nights for American soldiers and citizens alike was the Empire of Japan and, specifically, the Imperial Japanese Navy.

In the opening months of the war, that potent naval force had successfully attacked a strategic chain of sovereign nations and territories across the Pacific from Hawaii to Hong Kong and Darwin to Djakarta.

On the West Coast, including the waters around Catalina, the Japanese Navy manifested itself for the most part in the form of three I-class submarines that did the tiger's share of the damage: I-17, I-19 and I-21.

And while there are no recorded accounts of enemy submarine action directly involving Catalina, the activities of these submarines had a direct effect on the people of Catalina and no doubt kept regular surveillance on the activities here in Avalon. One can only imagine how many nights these submarines surfaced outside of the harbor trying to catch a glimpse of any military or commercial activity that might present a target.

The local action began on Christmas Eve 1941 in the San Pedro Channel between Catalina and the mainland when submarine I-19 under the command of Captain Nahara Shogo fired a torpedo at the merchant ship *S.S. Barbara Olson* on its way to San Diego.

Luckily, the torpedo missed, but Shogo and his crew had more success later in the day with a lumber-carrying ship called the *S.S. Absaroka* only about a mile off Point Fermin. As with the *Barbara Olson*, the submarine's first torpedo missed. But a second one was fired that hit the *Absaroka* just aft of her starboard beam, spinning her off course and knocking three deckhands into the sea.

A fourth seaman—Joseph Ryan—was trying to pull his three shipmates from the water when a lashing holding a stack of lumber on deck broke loose. The lumber tumbled overboard "like a man throwing matchsticks into the air" taking Ryan overboard with it. Ryan was killed instantly—the only fatality in the attack.

Thanks to compartmentalization of the ship's holds, the *Absaroka* did not sink and was towed to the beach below the cliffs at Fort MacArthur and although the Navy attempted to find and depth charge the perpetrator, the Japanese submarine slipped away undamaged.

Despite the attack on the *Absaroka* occurring within sight of Point Fermin, the entire event was successfully kept secret throughout the entire war. To this day, in fact, many people who were living in Los Angeles at the time are unaware of the attack on the *Absaroka*.

But one Catalina Islander had his own story to tell about the incident.

Like young men and women around the nation, the late Catalina Islander Bill White had just joined the U.S. Navy and was preparing to ship out to the South Pacific. His father Wilbur, it just so happened, was mayor of Avalon at the time and had made arrangements with the government for his son to fly to the Island one last time before heading off to war.

I interviewed Bill about his flight to the Island a few months before he passed way for my documentary *Wings Across the Channel*.

"It was a very interesting flight," said Bill, "because when we got mid-channel, the pilot of the plane started circling and circling and he turned to me and the rest of the passengers and said 'you are not to say a word about what you see below.'"

In the sea below them was the crippled freighter being kept afloat by a small fleet of ships and work boats. "We saw the Wilmington Transportation tug boats with pumps and everything trying to keep her from sinking," said Bill. "That really brought the war pretty close to home."

Bill's father Wilbur had a much closer encounter with an enemy submarine—possibly I-19—later in the war; an encounter that could have been disastrous had it not been for inclement weather conditions.

Because tourism to the Island had been cut off shortly after the attack on Pearl Harbor, Catalina Islanders had very little opportunity to make a living. One of the ways that they could do this was fishing.

The Navy—realizing the need of Islanders to make some cash while at the same time understanding their own need for vast quantities of food for their military operations around the world— would supply all the diesel and gasoline for local fishing boats at no charge. The Navy would then in turn buy all the fish caught by the locals.

"My father owned a sport fishing boat," said Bill, adding that he and his friend Eric Wilcox would often power out into the channel between Catalina and San Clemente Island to fish for albacore.

"One morning they went out in a very dense fog and all of a sudden there was a curtain of fog that lifted and they were headed straight into a Japanese submarine that was recharging its batteries on the surface in the early morning hours."

At that point, Bill's father did what any sensible man would do under the circumstances: He wheeled his vessel around and made a hasty retreat back into the fog bank before anyone on the submarine could react—an act that almost certainly saved both their lives.

Although enemy submarine activity began to subside within the first few months of the war, there were still a few tricks up the sleeves of the Japanese commanders, and the collective nerves of millions of Southern Californians would still be frayed for many months to come.

THE BATTLE OF LOS ANGELES

One of the most bizarre and amazing events ever to take place in the history of Southern California occurred in the wee early morning hours of February 25, 1942. And yet "The Battle of Los Angeles"—as it would come to be called—has remained one of the most misunderstood events in our history, possibly because it turned out that this "battle" was entirely one-sided and because—to this day—no one is entirely sure just exactly what happened.

It all started at about 1:30 a.m. when—according to the U.S. Government's 1983 publication *The Army Air Forces in World War II*—military radar picked up an "unidentified target 120 miles west of Los Angeles." The object was reported as "large" and travelling at an "exceedingly high rate of speed."

Because the attack on Pearl Harbor had occurred only three months earlier, the public's nerves were already a-jangle and it didn't help matters that only the night before, Japanese submarine I-17 had surfaced off the coast of Santa Barbara just long enough to lob a few shells at the Ellwood oil storage facility.

Fearing that this may be the start of an expected Japanese attack on the West Coast, anti-aircraft batteries around the Los Angeles area were put on alert.

At 2:15 a.m., a city-wide blackout was ordered in the Los Angeles area. Shortly after that, when the object would have been fairly close to Catalina Island, the unidentified target "vanished" from the radar.

At a few minutes past 3 a.m., anti-aircraft batteries fired four shots into the air in response to several accounts of local residents reporting a "large object" over Santa Monica airspace. Those first salvos were all that were needed for the rest of the batteries in Los Angeles to "erupt like a volcano."

For the next hour, pandemonium reigned and artillery shells rained as AAA fire lit up the sky in an effort to destroy the "enemy planes" that a number of people claimed to have seen. When it was over and the smoke had cleared, no one was quite sure what had happened nor, despite the radar blips, if there ever had been any objects in the sky at all.

The only damage from the event occurred from friendly fire in the form of shrapnel from the falling AAA shells. Several buildings were destroyed in the maelstrom and six civilians were killed outright or died of heart attacks attributed to the event.

Not surprisingly, a UFO component began to emerge to this story in later years; something that wouldn't have occurred to anyone in 1942. It was never determined what the large object was that had been initially sighted and skeptics later wrote it off to radar malfunction or possibly the presence of a weather balloon.

After the war, we learned that while the Japanese had been planning a limited attack on the Los Angeles area, they apparently had nothing to do with the Battle of Los Angeles. On Christmas Day 1941, the Empire of Japan had actually come within hours of a low-level attack on the city of Los Angeles, but by February of 1942 they had cancelled their plans and withdrawn many of their submarines from the West Coast.

FORTRESS CATALINA

For nearly a year after the attack on Pearl Harbor and in the face of a prohibition on all tourism to the Island (and therefore the primary means of making a living), the handful of residents that remained on Catalina led a Spartan existence.

Supplemented by whatever savings they had, residents turned to Victory gardens, hunting, fishing and the gathering of wild fruit to make ends meet during that bleak year of 1942. All the while they endured frequent air raid drills and nightly "blackouts" where the slightest sliver of light emanating from their homes would earn them a visit from the local Block Warden.

Desperate to pump economic life into his little colony on the Pacific, and mindful of Catalina's strategic value to the war effort, Philip Wrigley approached the varied branches of the U.S. military and offered them a place to set up operations.

First came the United States Coast Guard, which turned the Isthmus into a training station boasting more than 150 permanent officers, instructors and support personnel. Collectively, they mentored up to 90 recruits at a time in the laws of the sea and the weapons of war. It was the first military installation on Catalina Island since the Civil War.

Out in the hills, it was the U.S. Army Signal Corps that put together a series of gun emplacements, bunkers and a tiny village of barracks, mess halls and latrines known as Camp Cactus, much of which survives to this day, albeit in an advanced stage of decay.

Their job was to act as point men for the entire West Coast of the United States to (hopefully) detect the approach of enemy ships and submarines. Many were the lonely soldiers who passed the long, magical night beneath the Ben Weston stars or amid a chorus of crickets on the windswept headlands of China Point. Vigilantly, these silent sentries peered out to sea in search of any flash of light or any 3 a.m. glimpse of the conning tower of an enemy submarine.

But these coastal guardians didn't have to rely solely on their eyes to spot the enemy. They were aided in their efforts by that most secret and revolutionary technology known as RADAR. Used to great advantage by Britain's Royal Air Force during the Battle of Britain, RADAR technology was being put to good use in America as well and it is believed that Catalina Island was one of the first locations where it was used by U.S. forces.

The most prominent and visible branch of the military on the Island during the war was the United States Maritime Service, that branch of the government charged with running the nation's merchant fleet. Informally known as the "Merchant Marines," the officers and crew that propelled these ships around the world were in short supply in the opening salvos of the war and in October of 1942 the Maritime Service opened the Avalon Training School, effectively taking over the entire town of Avalon for their purposes.

Hotels, including the luxurious St. Catherine Hotel at Descanso Beach, were the primary living quarters for these trainees and various locations around town were converted to training facilities.

Part of the training "fun" for these cadets included learning how to swim through burning gasoline—a show they put on in the waters of Descanso Bay.

Dick Kellogg was one of those trainees and remembers well his turn at learning this skill. "You might think offhand that you could never do such a thing," said Dick. "They taught you to push the oil or the gasoline away from you. To this day I can still taste the gasoline in my mouth and all over my face and in my eyes."

Maneuvers were conducted up at the golf course, Stewards Department trainees learned their maritime culinary techniques in the kitchen at the St. Catherine and Engine Department trainees practiced on a fully-operational reciprocating steam engine located in Descanso Canyon.

Although U.S. Navy crews known as the Navy Armed Guard actually operated the guns aboard our merchant ships during the war, it was incumbent upon the semi-civilian Merchant Marines to also learn how to defend those ships should the Armed Guard be incapacitated in battle.

To achieve these ends, Casino Point bristled with a battery of 20mm anti-aircraft guns and non-firing 3-inch and 5-inch artillery put there for training purposes. Those awkward-looking cement pads that one still sees around the seawall at the Casino are the remnants of those gun emplacements and occasionally a SCUBA diver will still come up with a spent shell or two.

While most Islanders were quite aware of the presence on the Island of the Coast Guard, the Army Signal Corps and, of course, the Merchant Marines, it wasn't until after the war was over that they learned of a fourth group with whom they had unwittingly shared their island home.

By its very nature, this particular organization had kept its presence completely secret from everyone, save those who had a "need to know"...

THE MYSTERIOUS O.S.S.

Of the four branches of the military that established a presence on Catalina during World War II, none matches the mystique of the legendary O.S.S., an organization so secret that I'll wager you don't even know what O.S.S. stands for. And in the true spirit of this book, the presence of the "Office of Strategic Services" on the Island comes complete with its own hint of the paranormal, as you will see.

Toyon Bay was first leased to the O.S.S. in 1943, but it wasn't until June of 1944 that training operations actually began there. Operatives participated in myriad training activities and often spent weeks in the hills living off the land as part of their training, which no doubt meant lots of goat meat sandwiches.

Under the command of General William J. "Wild Bill" Donovan, operatives were prepared to land behind enemy lines during the Burma Campaign mainly in an effort to recruit locals to help the Allies wage war against the Japanese occupiers. Because Japanese troops were so despised in that region, the O.S.S. agents usually had little difficulty in getting recruits.

Catalina O.S.S. agents were instrumental in enlisting the services of groups as varied as the famed Kachin Rangers to real-life headhunters from the jungles of Southeast Asia.

Of special note at the Catalina O.S.S. base was the training of "Detachment 101," a group of Japanese-American volunteers, at least four of whom had come straight from internment camps on the West Coast.

In the closing months of the war, the Catalina O.S.S. base became headquarters for "Operation Napko." Like Detachment 101, Operation Napko involved the training of Koreans and Korean-Americans for similar behind-the-line operations on the Korean Peninsula and even the Japanese mainland itself. Unlike Detachment 101, however, the end of the war spelled the end of Operation Napko before any of the operatives were deployed.

And now for the part you've all been waiting for: Although it wasn't considered "paranormal" at the time, it is believed that the controversial technique known as "Remote Viewing" was practiced at Toyon Bay during the war.

Though fantastic in concept, Remote Viewing is a simple idea in practice. Essentially, a group of people deemed as being "psychic" are put into a room and given a sheet of paper and a pencil. They are then instructed to draw a sketch of a "target" assigned by the group leader. This target can be anything from an object in the next room to an island on the other side of the world.

The military advantages of such a program should be obvious and as wild as this idea sounds, it wasn't wild enough for Britain's Royal Air Force, the CIA and, later, the U.S. Air Force to dabble in this borderline black art.

During the Battle of Britain, the UK's intelligence wing known as MI6, desperate to gain intelligence on German positions in this pre-satellite era, had experimented with Remote Viewing. The U.S. Air Force operated their own program called "Stargate Project" after picking it up from the CIA in the mid-1970s. While the jury is still out as to whether or not Remote Viewing is worth the paper it is sketched on, the U.S. Air Force apparently thought enough of it to keep the effort going into the 1990s.

In fact, the only reason the Air Force may have stopped using it was because of advances in satellite technology.

The reason that I suspect the O.S.S. may have been dabbling in Remote Viewing at Toyon Bay comes down to two operatives that trained there, E. Howard Hunt and Lucien Conein, both of whom became heavily involved in the CIA's Remote Viewing program after the war.

Considering the enormous military value Remote Viewing would lend to Allied Forces, and considering the oodles of things that were going on at Toyon Bay about which the world will never hear, it's not too much of a stretch, in my humble opinion.

Finally, before I finish this segment, I want to slip one more item into the light of day concerning the O.S.S. and it has to do with the very first story in this book called "The Ghost in the Grumman Goose."

If you haven't read that story, let me sum it up for you:

One fine day in 1947, Amphibian Air Transport pilot Robert Hanley was flying his passenger-laden Grumman Goose through thick cloud cover above Catalina. To make a long story short, which is probably what you want anyway, Hanley had lost his radio antenna to frost build-up and therefore had lost use of his radio. He and his passengers were just about to plow into Mt. Orizaba when a voice came over his "dead" headset telling him to "Turn to nine-zero degrees! TURN NOW!"

Hanley did as instructed and fortuitously missed Catalina's highest peak, sparing his life and the lives of his eight passengers.

Hanley had no explanation for the mysterious voice, but I have long suspected that it's quite possible that the O.S.S. (by then the CIA) may have still been operating out of the area and that the voice came not from a "ghost" but from a CIA agent watching him on radar.

I like to think that this anonymous operative may have risked his career and maybe even his freedom by betraying his position with his broadcast to Hanley; all because he couldn't bear to watch a plane crash into the mountains when it was within his power to prevent it.

(Hanley's missing radio antenna would probably not have been a factor, provided that his plane was close enough to the theoretical transmitter at Toyon Bay).

Was the CIA still working out of Toyon after the end of the war? Are they still here today, somewhere on the Island?

If, after the publication of this book, I disappear from the face of the earth, then I suppose we'll have our answer.

THE WRECK OF K-111

From the dusty, formerly Top Secret files of Catalina's "wartime mysteries" comes one of the more tragic events to occur on the Island, along with the mystery that still surrounds it.

As is often the case with military operations gone wrong, official versions can curiously differ from the eyewitness accounts of those who found themselves unfortunate participants.

Such was the case with the wreck of U.S. Navy airship K-111 in 1944; an event which claimed the lives of seven Navy airmen and remains to this day the worst aviation disaster in Catalina's history.

For most Islander's living on the Island during the Second World War, the war years were at once both dark and yet at the same time filled with a spirit of camaraderie and shared sacrifice.

Within weeks of the attack on Pearl Harbor, tourism to the Island was cut off completely, leaving most residents to fend for themselves and to quite literally live off the land.

Others, including those who joined the military, simply had to leave their island home and hope they could return one day when the lights went on again all over the world.

As noted in an early segment, Japanese submarines patrolled the waters around the Island and had some success in sinking or disabling a number of U.S. merchant ships in the area. With most of the U.S. fighter planes needed in the battle arenas of Europe and the Pacific, the Navy had employed the use of dirigible airships, or blimps, to unceasingly patrol the waters of the west coast as far south as Scammon's Lagoon in Baja California.

On the evening of October 17, 1944, airship K-111 was on routine patrol in search of enemy submarines. Due to a navigation error, the blimp found itself passing directly over a blacked-out Avalon at an altitude of under 1,500 feet.

According to the official Navy version, the navigation problem was further aggravated by foggy conditions. The result was the airship's collision with the ground near East Peak and its "immediate explosion," according to the Navy.

But in the early 1990s, then-Catalina Island Museum Curator Patricia Moore conducted an interview with the last survivor of the crash, Machinists Mate Ernst Jarke of Nebraska. Jarke had made it a point to make one last pilgrimage to the Island to pay his respects to his fallen shipmates before he himself passed on.

In the interview, which survives on cassette tape in the museum's oral history collection, Jarke recalls that the night was a clear, starry one—not the foggy one in the official Navy report.

Also, according to Jarke, the ship did not explode on impact. In fact, the airship came to a slow, screeching halt after first brushing through the trees. The collision was enough to tear off the ship's port engine, but did not cause an immediate explosion as the Navy report asserts.

After the first scrape, the crew jumped safely from the ship's gondola and all reconnoitered at the top of the hill where the disabled ship lay. It was only when they were all milling about the wreck that the fuel tanks exploded. In other words, contrary to the official Navy version, they had all survived the crash, but had the made the fatal mistake of sticking around too long.

Jarke and the his shipmates all fled for their lives. Some were killed instantly, including Captain Thomas Ralston who was incinerated before Jarke's eyes.

Although engulfed in flames himself, Jarke managed to escape by running along a goat trail. A number of Merchant Marines from Avalon raced to the scene and loaded the survivors—including Jarke—into pick-up trucks to be taken to the infirmary in Avalon.

Jarke spent the next eight months in the Avalon infirmary recovering from his burns, but by the end of the war he was back flying in the airship service.

He passed away in 2003 at the age of 86—the last survivor of one of Catalina's most tragic episodes.

THE INFAMOUS "DR. DEATH"

Would you believe that only 25 years ago Catalina Island was the scene of the highly covert assassination of a Nazi war criminal at the hands of a clandestine group of Nazi hunters?

That proposal was put forth in a book released in 2008 titled *Not Forgotten, Not Forgiven*, written by a Danny Baz, a former Israeli Air Force colonel. In the book, Baz asserts that he was personally involved in the hunt for Nazi physician Dr. Aribert Hein with a group of Nazi hunters known as "The Owl."

Known as "Dr. Death," Heim was a doctor at the Mauthausen concentration camp in Austria where he carried out deadly medical experiments on prisoners.

Heim reportedly fled Germany in 1962 after police began investigating him and was reported living in various parts of the world, including Europe, South America and even the Middle East.

According to Baz, Heim was tracked down to Canada in the early 1980s where Baz and his cohorts somehow managed to wrangle the aging doctor to Catalina Island where the Nazi was "tried and executed."

No location on the Island was given for this adjudication and sentencing and the whole affair was ridiculed by the espionage community. The famed Simon Wiesenthal Center, renowned for its tireless pursuit of Nazi war criminals, claimed that Baz's assertions were "pure fantasy." The CIA and the U.S. Department of Justice also mocked Baz's story as did Paris-based Nazi hunter Serge Klarsfeld who said it was a "total fantasy."

Heim's family, for their part, claimed that Aribert died "in poverty" in Argentina in 2006. However, for obvious reasons, such claims by family members are rarely given much credence.

Then in 2009, the *New York Times* and German television station ZDF located an Egyptian hotel where they claimed Heim spent most of his post-war life. An old briefcase filled with faded papers and documents—including a certified Egyptian death certificate—were obtained by the two media outlets. The paper trail all lead to the conclusion, they claimed, that the old Nazi died in Cairo on August 10, 1992, nearly 20 years ago.

So it would probably be safe to say that the case can now be closed on the infamous "Dr. Death."

But then again...

The actual remains of Heim have never been found, so even some Nazi hunters are reluctant to completely give the case up.

Then there's the story that a life-long Catalina Islander told me about a Nazi-issued German passport that was found hidden in the walls of the old Glidden Bungalows on Avalon's west side when that building was being torn down in the 1980s. The name on the passport and the whereabouts of that passport has been long forgotten.

Like many of the Island's mysteries, we may never know the answer.

THE "CHINESE" MISSILE

It seems that once or twice a year, Catalina Island grabs national or international headlines for some reason or other, flattering or otherwise.

In this era of 24-hour news cycles, it is often something that thrusts our island paradise into the headlines at supersonic speeds. Such was the case on November 8, 2010, when a routine traffic report from a KCBS television crew suddenly morphed into a story worthy of a Tom Clancy novel.

Just about sundown on that day, CBS cameraman Gil Leyvas was taping from his lofty perch in the television station's news chopper when he noticed a billowing contrail fiercely blazing through the western sky about 10 miles off Catalina's West End. At the head of the contrail, glinting in the sun, was what appeared to be the craft responsible for all the commotion.

Leyvas dutifully turned his camera to the object and recorded for posterity the aerial phenomenon. The image was instantly picked up by the station and broadcast live, eliciting gasps of astonishment from the anchor crew.

Before the object was out of sight and the contrail dissipated, speculation began over just exactly what the object—a debate that continues to this day.

Both the Navy and Air Force immediately insisted they had no connection with the object, stating that they were not performing any military operations in the area at the time. Likewise, the North American Air Defense Command—whose job it is to make sure all such activities are monitored—claimed that the craft was not the result of any activity by anyone's military, including ours. No one had any idea where the object came from.

On the tamer side of the speculation brouhaha, a number of people of the skeptical persuasion declared the object was likely no more than an airliner departing LAX on its way across the Pacific, an idea that was quickly shot down the next day by Doug Richardson, editor of *Jane's Missiles and Rockets*.

In a report from *The Times* of London, Richardson declared that he had little doubt what the object was: "It's a solid propellant missile," he said. "You can tell from the efflux (smoke)."

Richardson went on to say it could have been either a ballistic missile launched from a submarine or perhaps a defensive anti-missile weapon.

Since the event occurred at the same moment that President Obama happened to be on a trip to the Far East, speculation immediately turned to the notion that the object was a Chinese missile brazenly launched off our most populous section of our West Coast as an embarrassment—or perhaps threat.

Despite the high profile nature of the event and the fact that it occurred in such close proximity to major civilian and military tracking installations, no consensus was ever reached as to just exactly what the object was. All sides are sticking to their stories and no similar event has occurred since (thereby arguing against the airliner theory).

While the origin of the mystery missile remains unknown, we do know that its ultimate destination was that shadowy-bound volume of mysteries that makes up Catalina's Twilight Zone.

?!

Fibs

Over the past century, a number of legends have grown around Catalina's history that upon further scrutiny have proven to be untrue. Nevertheless, they continue to be repeated as truth in local literature, on organized tours and even by many Island residents themselves. Here are but a few.

FIB NUMBER 1:
GAMBLING IN THE CASINO

Of the myriad myths surrounding Catalina Island, no doubt the most prevalent one is the notion that the Avalon Casino was once (or perhaps still is) a gambling casino. Imagine that.

While I've never known any Islanders who believed that, it's certainly not unreasonable for visitors to assume it's true. After all, why else would anyone call a building a "casino" if there wasn't gambling within its walls?

"I'll bet ya twenty bucks there's never been any gambling in this building," is usually my initial answer when asked this question. After the guffaws have stopped, I explain that there is not now, nor has there ever been, gambling allowed in the building and that it is used today in much the same way as it was the day it opened: a magnificent ballroom at balcony level and a fabulous movie theater at ground level.

But the question lingers, why the name "casino"?

The boilerplate answer we give to the puzzled visitor is that the word "casino" is an Italian word that means "a gathering place". I've never really felt that this response goes far enough because, for one thing, the Italian word "casino" actually has a number of different meanings and connotations (including "brothel"!), only one of which loosely refers to a "club" or "lodge".

And although coming up with the "gathering place" response may satisfy us, it still leaves the visitor confused and perhaps feeling a little tricked, especially if they came all the way out here to gamble (and I have met such people before).

"OK, so I forgot to pack my Oxford Dictionary of English Etymology," they say. "But everyone knows that any establishment in America called a 'casino' is used for gambling. What gives?"

The best overall answer to this I've devised is, quite simply, that in 1920s America when our Casino was built, the term "casino" was not used exclusively for gambling establishments. In those days, a "casino" could conceivably be any kind of large entertainment area with dancing, movie theaters, penny arcades, and so forth; an establishment akin to our modern day malls and gallerias, I suppose.

In other words, in 1929, if you were to tell someone you were going to a casino, they wouldn't automatically assume you were going someplace to gamble.

It wasn't until the late 1940s, I tell them, that the term "casino" began to be used exclusively for gambling establishments, at least in the United States. It all began in 1947 when a gentleman named Bugsy Segal opened the legendary Flamingo hotel and casino in a then-barren patch of Nevada desert that the world would come to know as Las Vegas. Ever since then, the terms "casino" and "gambling" have been synonymous.

Why haven't we changed the name? Well, since it's not really our fault that the definition of the word "casino" has evolved over the years into something it wasn't before, it's not really incumbent on us to change the name of our iconic landmark to fit the times.

By this point, most visitors are satisfied with my answers, although some insist that—for consistency—we turn the building into a genuine gambling casino in order to conform to the modern-day definition.

My usual response is, "I'll bet ya twenty bucks they'll never allow gambling in this building."

FIB NUMBER 2:
THE REMOVAL OF MR. WRIGLEY'S BODY

If you read the chapter on "Wartime & Military Mysteries," you know that the early months of World War II on the Island were nail-biting, to say the least, for the residents who stayed here. Tourism to the Island came to a complete halt and even travel to the Island for residents was severely restricted. Those who stayed on the Island endured years of air raid warnings and nightly blackouts for the duration of the war.

Given this angst-filled existence, it's not surprising that it gave birth to one of the Island's more prominent myths: that the body of William Wrigley, Jr., interred at the Wrigley Memorial in upper Avalon Canyon in 1934, was removed during the opening months of the war in apprehension of a possible Japanese takeover of the Island.

But although Mr. Wrigley's remains were eventually removed from Catalina to the mainland, the truth is that it didn't happen until long after the Japanese were considered a threat to the Island. In fact, it didn't happen until December 14, 1946, more than a year after the end of the war.

Our story begins with the death in 1932 of William Wrigley, Jr., and his desire to be interred on one of the great loves of his life, Catalina Island. Initially, the family planned to construct a memorial and family cemetery at Buena Vista Point near the Wrigley Mansion, but the location was changed shortly afterward to upper Avalon Canyon. Construction began on the new memorial that would come to be known as the Wrigley Memorial & Botanic Garden and it was there, in 1934, that Mr. Wrigley was first interred.

It had originally been the plan of the Wrigleys to have all family members eventually interred at the Memorial. In fact, the little tiled alcoves that one still sees on the top level of the Memorial were to be used for this purpose. But the plan was abandoned by Phillip K. Wrigley, the son of William Wrigley, Jr., for a variety of reasons after the war.

Part of the reason that the myth may have begun was the clandestine way in which the removal of Mr. Wrigley's remains was conducted in 1946. Although the family had publicly begun plans to move the remains as early as 1940, the war intervened and construction was delayed. When the move was finally made it was done with as little ceremony as possible and most Islanders weren't even aware of it until sometime afterwards.

Islander Chuck Liddell's father, Orville, was for many years one of the top brass in the Santa Catalina Island Company. From 1945 to 1960 he served as Chief Engineer in charge of all maintenance, road work, and assorted construction projects.

"As I recall my father telling me," said Chuck, "nobody knew about the body being removed until after the fact."

Orville told his son that on the appointed date the steamer *S.S. Avalon* made a trip to the Island, arriving at midnight. "The side (of the ship) opened up," he said, "and a hearse came out and went up to the Mausoleum. After picking up Mr. Wrigley's body, the hearse went back to the *S.S. Avalon* and the ship blew its horn once before going back to the mainland. The next morning the town woke up and found out the body had been removed."

No one is exactly sure how the World War II myth began, but like most legends it probably just slowly developed over the years. As memories faded and residents who had lived here during and shortly after the war moved or passed away, it slowly took on a life of its own and became part of Island lore.

FIB NUMBER 3:
THE CHIMES TOWER AND WRITER ZANE GREY

Forty-seven times each day, we hear her sweet tones calling out to us from the hilltop on Avalon's west side, tolling the time of day in 15-minute increments. On special occasions (or sometimes for no particular reason at all) we are treated to a town-wide *concerto* of old standards from "Home on the Range" to "Avalon."

Since 1925, the Chimes Tower on the town's west side has served as Avalon's timekeeper, entertainer and one of Catalina's more prominent cultural icons. At Christmas time, carols are regularly chimed to busy afternoon shoppers and in days-gone-by the peal of the chimes welcomed the daily arrivals of the steamers with "Avalon" and saw them off each afternoon with "Vaya Con Dios" and other farewell tunes.

But clouding this legacy is an undeserved myth whose origins are a matter of speculation. That myth is that Ada Wrigley intentionally built the Chimes Tower where it is, near the Zane Grey Pueblo, in an effort to annoy writer Grey because of some supposed animosity between the two.

This interesting legend seems to be indelibly imprinted in Catalina's "fiblore" to the extent that it is still regularly told to visitors, including on formal Avalon tours, and is occasionally even parroted in the international press.

A recent travel article on Catalina published on the *Islands* magazine website, in fact, sums this tale up nicely: "According to local stories," the segment begins, "[Ada Wrigley] was so disgusted by Zane Grey's habit of noisily hanging out late with his Tuna Club cronies, she arranged for the Chimes Tower to go up just outside Grey's home, where it rang out the time every 15 minutes, beginning at 8 a.m."

To begin with, anyone who personally knew Mr. and Mrs. Wrigley or who has studied the history of their relationship with the people of Catalina knows that the idea that Ada Wrigley would go to such retaliatory lengths against anyone—regardless of how she felt about the person—is preposterous, to put it mildly.

The Grey family evidently concurs. Michael Shehabi has for many years been manager, historian and guardian over the Zane Grey Pueblo, now one of Avalon's charming hotels. "It's a rumor in town I've heard from day one," he said. "In my personal opinion, I love the Chimes Tower. It blends in with the Pueblo."

Zane Grey's son Loren, himself a writer and noted educational psychologist, spent many an hour in conversation with Michael in the hotel's office until Loren's death in 2007. The legend of the Chimes Tower's origins occasionally came up in these conversations.

"I was very close to Loren," said Michael. "I have personally asked him (about the legend) and he kind of laughed," he said,

107

adding that Loren told him that his father "got along pretty well with the Wrigleys."

Michael has also posed the same question to Lee Grey, Zane's nephew. "He doesn't believe it either."

"Claiming that the Wrigleys would do something like that makes them look bad," said Michael. "They wouldn't have done such a thing."

The origins of the myth may have something to do with a dispute that Zane Grey had at one point with the Tuna Club, of which he was a member. This dispute was little more than an argument over whether or not the wife of another Tuna Club member should receive credit for catching a particularly large tuna. What's important to our story is not so much the dispute itself, but that Mrs. Wrigley was on the opposing side of the beef.

While it's highly unlikely that such a disagreement between Zane Grey and Ada Wrigley would have caused any lasting damage, it is certainly possible that over the years and decades this dispute over a tuna could have spawned the Chimes Tower myth, thereby making it—quite literally—another Catalina "fish story."

FIB NUMBER 4:
THE HOTEL ST. CATHERINE'S DEMISE

The beautiful Hotel St. Catherine in Descanso Canyon was a Catalina icon for many decades, beginning with its construction in 1918. The project was initiated by the then-owners of the Island, the Banning family, in a somewhat desperate bid to help the Island's economy following the devastating 1915 fire.

While the opening of the hotel was indeed a prestigious shot in the arm for the Island, ultimately it failed to revive the Island's tourist trade in the way the Bannings had hoped and in 1919 they turned the keys to the Island over to William Wrigley, Jr., ushering in a new era in Catalina's history.

Over the next 25 years, the St. Catherine played host to a number of celebrities and other well-to-dos that came to enjoy Catalina's fun and sun.

The fib surrounding the demise of the hotel begins with the Second World War, when the United States Maritime Service set up a training station in Avalon. With tourism to the Island suspended for the duration of the war, the hotels around Avalon became living quarters for the Maritime Service trainees and a myth was born.

Because of the St. Catherine's extensive kitchen and pantry areas, it was decided to house and train cadets mostly from the Maritime Service's Stewards Department, that cadre of a ship's personnel charged with cooking, cleaning and general shipboard housekeeping.

The St. Catherine was finally demolished in 1966 and this particular Catalina fib holds that it was the havoc wreaked by those Maritime Service trainees during the war that, 20 years later, resulted in the decision to raze the old beauty.

Now, having spent some time in the Merchant Marine myself, I've always been a little irked at the accusation that my fellow shipmates could be responsible for the destruction of such a beautiful hotel. Not that the implication is entirely unjustified. Merchant Marines aren't exactly the kind of people you want to invite *en masse* to your baby shower. But the wartime training of the Maritime Service cadets was done in very military fashion and cleanliness and order was the rule.

Long-time Avalon resident and former Maritime Service trainee Dick Kellogg was there for several months during the war. "I'd like to say that that really is not the case," he said, referring to his fellow trainees as being the culprits. "When I was there, we had to take very good care of the hotel. We had inspection every Saturday morning— white glove inspection. We really had to clean the place up and keep it straight.

"After the trainees left, that hotel ran for 20 years before they tore it down," he said. "Now, I don't know where this tale ever started, but I just wanted to say that I don't believe it."

It was in the post-war years that many of the hotel's rooms were reconfigured for monthly tenants; a situation that—as any hotel manager will tell you—can greatly speed up wear and tear on a building.

"They had actually used it for some housing ," said Rudy Piltch, adding that rooms were reconfigured and kitchens added for month-to-month rentals. "But it was just getting very worn and not the kind of place people were going to want to stay in."

Rudy remembers the day in February 1966 when he watched as a crane complete with wrecking ball began demolishing the building. "Before they brought the wreckers in they did allow a lot of people from Avalon to come out and pick out what they wanted," he said.

In addition to the post-war wear and tear, the decision to raze the building had just as much to do with the economics of the times and the changing travel tastes of the American public.

With few exceptions, palatial hotels like the St. Catherine just weren't as popular as they had been before the war. The average American tourist couldn't afford to stay in such a place and those who could afford it now had a variety of new and more exotic destinations they could choose over Catalina.

Advances in aviation technology, for example, now gave the "jet set" the opportunity to fly to places like Honolulu or the previously-unknown Mexican fishing village of Puerto Vallarta; a destination popularized by the 1964 academy award-winning film *Night of the Iguana* starring Richard Burton and Ava Gardner.

ABOUT THE AUTHOR

Jim Watson is an author and filmmaker who has lived on Catalina Island since May of 1995. His award-winning documentary *Wings Across the Channel*, the story of the Golden Age of the seaplanes on Catalina, has aired on KCET-TV in Los Angeles, the nation's largest public television station, and he has appeared on the Discovery Channel's series *Sins & Secrets*.

He is also a freelance writer for the weekly *Catalina Islander* newspaper, including his column "Mysterious Island" which has been running since January of 2011.

Born in Pasadena, he was raised in Chico, California, and is a 1985 graduate of California State University, Chico.

JIM WATSON

Made in the USA
Monee, IL
23 July 2023